OK, INTRIGUING:
HELL YEAH!
AWESOMENESSOUS

Fifty-four humor essays that will force you to
unleash indulgence rumbles from your deepest
amusement precincts until your noggin detonates

David Tieck

Author of
The Embarrassing-Memory Murderer

OK, INTRIGUING: HELL YEAH! AWESOMENESSOUS
FIFTY-FOUR HUMOR ESSAYS THAT WILL FORCE YOU TO
UNLEASH INDULGENCE RUMBLES FROM YOUR DEEPEST
AMUSEMENT PRECINCTS UNTIL YOUR NOGGIN DETONATES

iUniverse books may be ordered through booksellers or by contacting:

iUniverse LLC
1663 Liberty Drive
Bloomington, IN 47403
www.iuniverse.com
1-800-Authors (1-800-288-4677)

Because of the dynamic nature of the Internet, any web addresses or links contained in
this book may have changed since publication and may no longer be valid. The views
expressed in this work are solely those of the author and do not necessarily reflect the
views of the publisher, and the publisher hereby disclaims any responsibility for them.

Any people depicted in stock imagery provided by Thinkstock are models,
and such images are being used for illustrative purposes only.
Certain stock imagery © Thinkstock.

ISBN: 978-1-4917-4506-9 (sc)
ISBN: 978-1-4917-4507-6 (hc)
ISBN: 978-1-4917-4508-3 (e)

Library of Congress Control Number: 2014915151

Printed in the United States of America.

iUniverse rev. date: 09/30/2014

Cover design by
Nick Day and David Tieck

'Please stop using me as an example'
Quotes

Get this out of the way now

You know the deal, this book is largely fiction, only some of the celebrities in this book gave me permission to write about them, some of the scientific facts in this book are less 'facts' and more 'really super strong hunches', and not everything that happens in this book is 'true', some of it (particularly the purely fictional parts) I plumb just made up with my brain. Therefore if any of these stories resemble your life, or people you know, well then it is purely coincidental, and frankly freakishly coincidental. Wait, are you my long lost and unknown other me, living in a parallel universe whom I sometimes see in my dreams, and know to be my other me rather than myself because you can fly and yet I cannot? What is flying like man? How's the apocalypse working out? It looks unbelievably violent and hellish, but as a flyer you just get to watch, oh man you're so lucky. I wish I were you. Was sex with Emma Watson as good as it seemed? How are book sales on your side? Oh that's right, I remember, from that one dream, that the apocalypse was caused by people not telling enough of their friends to buy your book, leading to a world wide lack of Hell Yeah awesomenessous, resulting in death to just about everyone but you. I'm sure we won't make the same mistake on this side. See you soon dude, oh and good luck fighting Ghomoragon again tonight!

Contents

Foreword

by David Tieck

When I was asked by David Tieck to write the foreword for his book I couldn't keep the smile off my face. Out of all the myriad of celebrities and influential men and women from around the world that David could have easily gotten to write his foreword, and I mean really EASILY could have gotten, he chose me, ME! Just *think* of the people David could have *easily* gotten, like that he would barely have needed to even ask, but chose not to:

J.K Rowling

Tina Fey

Conan O'Brien

Dave Barry

Barrack Obama

Kurt Cobain

Russell Crowe

Jeremy Irons

Jena Malone

Andy Day's identical twin brother Nick

Dakota Fanning

J.D. Salinger

Craig Ferguson

A bowl of Cereal

Norm Macdonald

Michael Ian Black

Eric Cartman

Saddam Hussein's long lost love child Trevor
Ricky Gervais
W. Axl Rose
A blonde girl
Jean-Michel Basquiat
An historical figure

It's a pretty impressive list, especially since they are people who have all earned a line just to themselves, and to also be listed in a sexy way all centered and phallic like that, and I mean it is simply a who's who list of authors, comedians, actors, artists, scholars, miscreants, marsupials and all round David Tieck fans, and yet he chose me. I've had a smile on my face since he asked me, I have a smile on my face right now, and I have a clear vision in my mind of smiling in the future while thinking about the smiling I am doing now, all while smiling thinking about the smiling I was doing when he asked me.

And that's the thing with David Tieck; he makes you smile. I would say that if there is one thing David loves more than anything else it is making people smile. Most people tend to say the thing they love more than anything else is 'love' or 'sex' or 'cheese' or 'eating fondue out of my lover's vagina', but not David Tieck, he loves to make people smile. Frankly I doubt you could find a human alive who hasn't smiled once or twice because of David Tieck, and if you ask me that's magical. Consider this list of people David has made smile:

David Letterman
David Duchovny
David Beckham
David Lynch
Larry David
David Gilmore
King David of Jerusalem
The King of Sweden
A blonde girl

Captain Caveman
Chuck Palahniuk
Nick Day's identical twin brother Andy
Crocodile Dundee
Taylor Swift's hair
A scientist
Saddam Hussein's long lost love child Trevor's long lost wife Carmel
An empty bottle of beer
Steve Martin
Oprah
David Bowie
An historical figure

Thinking of all the people David Tieck has made smile really makes me smile. Sometimes I just sit and smile at the thought of their smiles. In fact I have a clear vision in my mind of smiling in the future while thinking about all the smiling people are doing because of David Tieck right now, all while smiling thinking about the smiling I was doing when I first smiled because of David, and if you ask me that's magical.

So I hope you enjoy this book. Between you and me this David Tieck fellow may well just be a crazy genius whose bafflingly brilliant brain, profoundly absurd observations, and unyieldingly modest and benevolent take on the world may just detonate your noggin so hard they'll be picking bits of your brain off your *neighbors* ceiling. He may even be worthy of featuring on a future list of who's who of amazing people such as above. Let's try it out just for fun, and see how it feels:

King Henry the VIII
Thomas Edison
Dave Chappelle
Jason Priestly
Uncle Jesse
The NSW Waratahs Rugby Team
Mr Bean

David Tieck
Steffi Graf
Hayley from Paramore
A wet paint sign
Little Miss Neat
A fireplace
Saddam Hussein's long lost love child Trevor's
friends Andy and Nick Day
Monkey Magic
A used napkin
Albert Einstein
Winston Churchill
A blonde girl
An historical figure

Well if you ask me that feels pretty God damn right. And wow, what a list to be included on! It's a who's who list of actors, sportsman, inventors, rapscallions, Davids, woodland creatures and magicians, and I think David is not just *maybe* worthy of a future list like that, but nay DESTINED for it. Frankly it is almost a dead cert, and honestly, thinking about that, well it just makes me smile, and if you ask me, that's magical.

Foreword Two

by Kurt Cobain's Angel

When I was asked to write the foreword to David Tieck's book, the first thing I asked was 'who the fuck is David Tieck?' But then it was explained to me that David was a man who didn't much care for my music while I was alive, thinking it was for whiny juveniles, but who then learned to appreciate and love it after my death, oh and he claims to be a writer. Well great, thanks David!

I had zero inclination to help him, I know nothing of his work, and as far as I know he may be some sort of asshole who uses other people's names without their permission in a vain attempt of finding an unearned audience. I HATE people like that. But then, they told me I could tell all of you wonderful people about the marvelous place I live in now, a sweet little place you may know as 'heaven', and I thought 'fuck it'; if you get a chance like that then you take it.

And I've got to tell you - heaven is AWESOME!!!!!! I mean simply magnificent. The people are super friendly, the music is excellent, your hair turns blonde without even needing to bleach it, you only have to be super famous if you really, really want to, and the holes in your jeans magically fix themselves, so no more cold knees!

It's really a wonderful, humble and simple place to live – mobile cellular telephones do not yet have scrabble, so you're not distracted while driving, the most popular internet social networking site changes all the time, so you don't get hooked, certain sport teams that certain people support win more than some others at some times, and yet other different certain sports teams that other certain people support also win at times more than others, so surprise sporting outcomes can hit you at any time! Female pop stars are all attempting to out whore each other, different people have different political views than other people, there are no Spelling Nazis, Fashion Nazis, Coaster Nazis, Sand Castle Nazis, or even Nazi Nazis, more people are startled by random encounters with silverfish than silverback gorillas, squash is both a sport and a fruit, the carpet is all very plush, and a small percentage of the population speak with a really cute and funny accent they call 'Australian'.

The point is, I *highly* recommend it, heaven that is, not attempting an Australian accent, NO ONE who isn't Australian can pull it off, trust me I've tried and failed, and I'm an artistic genius.

Anyway, got to go, I have seventy two virgins I still have to work my way through, but oh, I should tell you just one more thing, I met this young man who calls himself 'Gandhi', and he has the most marvelous heroin I've ever tried- mmmwwwwah! You've *got to* try it! Ha ha, just kidding, in heaven EVERYTHING gives you a pleasure hit like heroin, eating broccoli, wearing an uncomfortable hat, getting hit by a train, you name it, I bet getting shot in the head even feels good here! Yaaaayyyy! Bye guys.

Foreword Three
by David Tieck

Well I feel like a shit now. You used me David Tieck, you already had a much bigger name lined up AND he was going to reveal what heaven is really like! You just wanted me to make an ass of myself, didn't you? Well I hope you die you prick. Oh and DON'T end up in heaven, which actually sounds wonderful, so thanks for finally providing infallible evidence that it's real, and finding out for us just how awesome it is, that's a tremendous public service bound to bring peace to people's minds around the globe, and make just about everyone a better person. But still, you used me, and I am the person who conjured up every wet dream you've ever had, and you know what? I'm not giving you anymore, yep, they're DONE! Fuck you, you fucking acid reflux spit. Oh I love that insult, it really makes me smile.

Foreword Four

by Kurt Cobain's Angel

OOOOk, 'acid reflux spit'? I do NOT want my good name to be associated with language that terrible. You really are a piece of shit David Tieck. Please remove my foreword immediately.

One

You better believe those are some kick ass credentials

Thanks Dave and Kurt for those kind words, I love you guys, you truly are my heroes, and I'll even say it, you are my equals, and that's high praise coming from me. Although I do also have to say that while Kurt Cobain and I may have a heap in common, there is one way in which we will always be different. Kurt you see was a small town boy, but unlike him I was always a city boy.

At least I *thought* I was a City Boy.

I had all the city credentials you see; I lived in a city for example, I enjoyed being in a city would be another example which would suggest I had City Boy credentials, and I enjoyed that I lived in a city would be yet another example of why I thought I had City Boy credentials. And usually you would think that three flawless credentials would be flawless proof that you are in fact what your credentials apparently prove you are. But really sometimes you don't know how much you *are* a City Boy until you meet a City Girl and you find out that in reality you have shitty city credentials.

The City Girl was really city. She lived in a city, which was one of my credentials that she shared, but she had other city credentials too, like she enjoyed being in the city, oh wait I had that one too, and yes, she enjoyed that she lived in the city, just like I proved above that I also did, but here is the thing, this City Girl had even *further* city credentials!

Like she *smelled* like the city, when she sweated she literally sweat city grime. And she cared enough to add her grime right back into the city, in a city supports me so I will support my city ring of help which was both beautiful and a credible City Girl credential.

Plus she *looked* like a city, by which I mean she was a cluster fuck of awesomenessous, by which I mean she was bad at doing her hair and putting on her make-up, and yet didn't care, just like a city doesn't care how the fuck its hair and make-up looks. And when you share something like that with a city then your City Girl credentials *shred* up the City Girl charts.

Her city credentials didn't end there no; fear not, she even had a *name* like a city! Her name was Constantine, which if a city was named, for example, 'Constantine City' that would be an awesome name for a city, and therefore an awesome city, which is why I considered her name to be a city like name and therefore yet another reason she could use as a City Girl credential.

That city would also have awesome sporting teams like the 'Constantine City Carnies' who would win games by tricking their opponents that the rules of the game are fair when in fact the ball doesn't even fit in the ring, or the 'Constantine City Carhorns', who would win games by being rude and obnoxious, or the 'Constantine City Cougars' who would be the laughing stock of the league after their fierce cat name has been turned into a name used for desperate horny middle aged women who want to get in three more fucks before their vaginas stop producing lubrication (that's the words of the people making fun of the Constantine City Cougars, not me). Plus even the word 'fierce' has been taken by fashion assholes and the like, and so no one would ever want to play for the Constantine City Cougars, which would mean they would end up with all the players black listed from other teams for beating up their wives, and urinating on little girls thinking they were toilets, so oh yeah, you better believe the Constantine City Cougars would play the game hard and with bone to pick, and I mean a literal bone, these guys would eat ribs for sure. Also there would be the 'Constantine City Caregivers', who it would turn out would be more of a charitable group that helps runaways than a sporting team per se, but some of those runaways would be running away from their fathers who play for the Constantine City Cougars, so you can probably see in this example how it all comes around. So yeah, you better believe being named Constantine gives you badass City Girl credentials. And they were credentials that this Constantine City Girl had in spade loads of city credential awesomeness.

But did her credentials end there? Of course the fuck not they fucking did not, and fuck you if you even thought her city credentials might cease to conglomerate out of her City Girl pores. Check this out - she even *lived* in a city. Oh wait, fuck, I've covered that one. Oh, no I got it, she also once showed me her vagina and it had steam coming out of it like a big city manhole! Manholes in small towns *don't* have steam coming out of them do they? You're God fucking damn it for fucking sure hell right they don't, so Hell Yeah you better believe that if a girl's vagina has steam coming out of it like a big city man hole then this chick has big ass City Girl credentials.

Is that the end of the credentials? Yes it is. Oh wait no it's not, she even once had sex with the mayor of a city, and when you work in city hall that means you've been *in* City Hall, and when you make love to Constantine that means you've been *in* Constantine, which means that in this little free flying fucking kick ass factoid, Constantine and City Hall have become one and the same, as in the mayor has been *in* both of them, and when you share an *in* with City Hall, you better fucking have faith in the reality that you have kick cunt City Girl credentials.

Lets take a moment to weigh up these facts:

My City Boy Credentials - I lived in the city, I enjoyed being in a city, I enjoyed that I lived in a city.

Her City Girl Credentials - She lived in a city, she enjoyed being in a city, she enjoyed that she lived in a city, she oozed grime like a city, she did her hair like a city, she was named like a fucking awesome city which would have awesome city sport teams, her vagina streamed steam like a city, and she practically WAS city hall, as in the mayor did his best work inside of her, and she even *lived* in a city.

It was clear, she was a City Girl but I was no City Boy. There was only one thing for it, I would have to leave the city, as my City Boy credentials were far too shitty for me to be pure City Boy, and as shitty as it was to leave the city, I knew I would return one day. I just had to. I mean apart from anything, I really wanted to taste that City Girl steam for myself, so if I want to be a City Boy the way I want to be, I guess it's clear – it's time I run for Mayor.

Two

Please don't do it

As your future Mayor (do they even have Mayors where you are?) I know exactly what you're thinking, and I am really sorry, but I don't think you should adopt a camel.

Yes, I know, there have been so many stories about the Middle-East on the news in the past decade or so, and you sit and watch and think 'terrorists suck, but those camels sure look cool' and you're right, they do look cool, but cool does not make an awesome pet I am afraid.

I agree with you, camels make a *unique* pet and being unique is good, but I promise you, many, many people are thinking of making the move for the camel ownership life right now, and if you also jump in and buy a camel, soon you'll find yourself whack bang in the middle of an ill-thought-out trend. Do you want your camel to turn into the equivalent of recent other well known ill-thought-out trends like a butterfly tattoo on your lower back, or a florescent microscope collection, or a replacement artificial hand where every finger is now a different sized Phillips head screw driver? No you don't. You can have your tattoo removed, throw out a florescent microscope, or cut off your hand yet again and get a cool hook instead, but with a camel you're stuck.

I am right with you, is a camel cute? Hell Yes, but cuteness fades, and you'll find yourself looking at baby camels in the pet store window thinking 'I wish my camel was still cute like that, my camel sucks'. No no, it *will* happen, and I know that doesn't mean you won't still love your camel, but it should be considered.

The other thing is, and this may shock you, but camels, as it turns out, make really, really awful pets. Trust me. And I know what you're thinking, you don't trust me, and you prefer facts, so ok: here are some facts you may not yet have thought about showing why camels make bad pets:

- They're kind of big. If you live in a studio apartment where the hell are you going to put it? Even if you have a courtyard or roof top garden, camels like to move around, and a restless camel is a horny camel, hey don't blame me, it's a fact, and if you thought horses were hung like horses, well camels are REALLY hung like horses (even female ones, camel clitoris is enormous!)
- They're not good eating, which means fifty years from now when it sadly passes away you're going to have to drag a big heavy body to the trash can rather than farming its body for meals, that's annoying AND wasteful.
- They have weird lumps on their backs, and if you have a pet with weird lumps people may think YOU'RE weird.
- In the desert the smell of a camel's ass can be a delightful distraction from the smell of sweaty unwashed Middle-Eastern people (by which I mean of course people who live in the Middle East of all races so I'm not racist), but in your apartment it just smells like camel ass (which is bad, if that wasn't clear). On the other hand camel breath may now become a delightful distraction from camel ass, but please trust me, this is NOT a good reason to adopt a camel for a pet.
- They only come in brown – BOOOOORING.

You know what? I feel like you are not yet convinced, so let me throw a curve ball at you. No, not one of those stupid metaphoric ones which just end up confusing people who are not big fans of sport (if you don't know sports - curve balls are a devious move designed to trick you and are popular in a myriad of sports, including baseball, tennis, ice-hocky, rock climbing and competitive sandal washing). But *I* mean a *literal* curve ball, because this unrelenting desire of yours to have a pet camel, even now, after I have PROVEN that camels are in fact an awful choice for a pet, has really started to get under my nerves, and as it happens, just as you were forming this camel desire I was working out how to position my wrist in just the right way so that I can now make a baseball curve when thrown from my hand towards something, and this is a very difficult thing to do, especially by someone with no access to high level baseball coaches (although it is relatively simple in rock climbing).

So can I throw a curve ball at you please? No? Fuck you. Enjoy your camel asshole.

Fun Camel Facts:

- There are a bunch of feral ones in the middle of Australia.
- They make awful pets.
- They can't throw curve balls.
- If you replace their hooves with artificial hands where every finger is now a different sized Phillips head screw driver they look super cool, and become a very practical pet, you cruel bastards.

Three

Notes from a guy with sex goals

Hello everyone, my name is Warren Clinder, and this is the story of my sexual life:

I was twenty-nine when I lost my virginity, which for a bachelor in the 1930s was quite young. The beautiful young lady's name was Angela, and rumor had it she'd already slept with *three* people, and she was only forty-two! Oh boy, it sure was neat to get the chance to meet such a slut to help me become a man.

Barbra came into my life three years later and we made love after only dating for seven months. I was starting to think I was quite the stud (which back then was a term reserved for horses, but I was very well endowed in the nose department, like freakishly big, so I certainly felt I had satisfactorily complimented myself).

After Barbra dumped me for being 'shit in bed' (how can one be excrement in bed? That never made sense to me) I found comfort in the arms of Cindy, all 400lbs of them (I only weighed the arms, I couldn't get her whole body on the scales, and besides I didn't want to do anything to make her feel uncomfortable about her weight). Keep in mind in those days men clamoured all over themselves for curvier women, and when those women turned us down the epically morbidly obese were the 116th next best thing, right between rabbits (hard to catch) and trees (splinters, ouch).

Sadly Cindy died during the act (sadly for her private cheese dealer). And I found myself at the ripe old age of thirty-seven (life expectancy was fifty two then, and I never was an confident fellow) and I was in a speakeasy one night when I optimistically started chatting to a fine beauty named Deidra and I found myself asking her out. She of course laughed in my face and then instructed a random man in the vicinity to beat me to near death, which he did with the glee of a school girl, and as I lay in hospital for the next two years (there was not yet a cure for thirty eight broken bones), I had plenty of good ol' thinking time and it occurred to me that had sweet Deidra responded positively to my attempts to woo her, my first four ladies I had made love to would have had first names beginning with A, then B, C & D!

It was a mighty fine thought, as I am sure you can imagine (apologies if you cannot, I understand that not every man has had such success with the ladies as me). It was such a nice thought in fact that it inspired a pact (Little known pact fact: all pacts are factual). I pacted that I would sleep with exactly twenty six ladies in my life, I know, a scandalous sum, that I am sure no other man would dare dream of, but it seemed fated (pacts are also fated, unless you make a pact to do something like start every day with sit-ups, that's not fated, it's stupid) and these twenty six women would have names starting with the letters A through Z, in order. It would be my greatest triumph (and only triumph, triumphs were difficult in those days).

That's how I found myself making love to the beautiful Diana, the one armed quadriplegic nurse who had recently had a bomb land on her in World War II (Although we called it 'that European shooty thing' at the time) (Oh and for your information the burns only made her *more* beautiful so shame on you).

We met in the rehabilitation ward of the hospital and when I asked if she would like to make love she replied 'I guess, I mean it's not like I have any feeling in my body, so I wont feel it,' ha ha, she sure did have a great sense of humor for a war victim.

Ethel came a few months later when by chance I was visiting my grandmother in the old folks home and Ethel was in there visiting her daughter, but after that things got lean for a while, I mean 'F' names were hard to come by in those days. Not like today with your fancy 'Felicitys', 'Fays', 'Felicias' and the like, in those days people respected their children enough not to give them crazy crap names! (Sorry for my language, but it makes me mad).

Thankfully things turned around thirty odd years later (life expectancy had improved greatly since the discovery of penicillin, and the cure for thirty eight broken bones). I was drafted into Vietnam after the army refused to believe that I was seventy-four and that there had been a clerical error, and so they sent me over where I had the pleasure of fornicating with a prostitute named Fung.

Now you would think that making love for the first time in thirty years would make me happy, but it turned out that these 'prostitutes' didn't *only* exist in Vietnam, and were in fact back in America also, and so I could have easily worked my way through the remaining letters with a crazy week in Vegas and spent my life seeking normal relationships or even a wife. But you know what? In old age you realize there is no point holding on to regrets, you're already putting so much effort into holding on to your bowels, so I gave up on the pact there and then. I realized I had bigger things to worry about now, important things, like the terrible music the damn kids now listened to, and the fact that my severely enlarged prostate made it very difficult to pee in the jungle while the Viet Cong shot at me, or the fact that my sergeant apparently needed to cross the letter 'W' off his old man gay sex A-Z sex goal.

Sex goals sure are great.

Four

It's just unbelievable

Thanks Warren, that sure was a swell story, I was about to say a practically fucking unbelievable story, but then I caught myself and had to scream for nearly using such an evil horrible vile word, and frankly, if you ask me, I think it's high time the word 'unbelievable' is banished from the English language. BANISHED.

I mean, consider this routine and highly familiar everyday conversation:

'Hello person I know'
'Oh hello person who knows me'
'Hello you too, oh you should check out this thingy I am aware of, but you may not yet be aware of…. it's *unbelievable!*'

Um um um um

'WHO THE HELL ARE YOU TO TELL ME WHAT I AM CAPABLE AND INCAPABLE OF *BELIEVING* you you you YOU BASTARD!' I want to yell.

Let's get this straight - for starters, please sure as hell don't expose me something that you *know* to exist and then tell me it's unbelievable. Are you genuinely trying to tell me that you think I am 'incapable' of *believing* something that you KNOW to exist? People believe all sorts of shit in this world that they don't 'know' exists, so don't you dare say to me 'this is unbelievable' about something that DOES exist - you arrogant condescending asshole. But more than that - 'WHO THE HELL ARE YOU TO TELL ME WHAT I AM CAPABLE AND INCAPABLE OF *BELIEVING* you you you YOU BASTARD!' I want to yell. I am capable of believing some pretty out there wacky shit, thank you very much. Don't believe me? Well check this out:

Monkey colonies, living in oxygen pods two miles under sea, living off bananas shipped down by black marlin, under the promise of monkey on land protection from black marlin predatory deep-sea fisherman. That's unbelievable right?

WRONG! No it's not, it's perfectly believable, in fact it is the reason I am scared of eating bananas.

Angels, no bigger than a freak baby mini flea, that come out of your butt when you fart, whose job it is to carry away the smell after the smell has lingered for the exact most horrific and/or funny amount of time. That's unbelievable right?

WRONG! It's the reason I always get horribly sad when I see someone attack a fart with bug spray.

Helicopters that fly upside down over the desert to make sure that all obnoxious and sticky beaked long necked animals are decapitated or at least not allowed to grow tall enough to make fun of the famous desert ghost who was upset because so many sticky beaked long necked animals made fun of his slightly below average human height, so he attempted to invent a solar powered hot air balloon, but failed so bad that he kicked a rock, and stubbed his toe so bad that the toe nail was chipped, and left him bitter and angry and incapable of feeling attractive in even the most expensive jeans, so he went to the desert and perished trying to use a cactus as pants, and died screaming 'I hate man made flying machines, why can't one help me for once???' That's unbelievable right?

WRONG! Um, sorry it's perfectly believable, and it's the plot of a movie I just sold to Disney.

Girl's who like sex as much as men, especially with longhaired, weird minded Australian men named Dave and want to track him down and have sex with him? That's unbelievable right?

Um no, well ok, that one is kind of unbelievable.

But wait, check this out, tiny angels that come out of underwater monkey farts and float up and morph into solar powered hot air balloons with slogans written on them that make girls horny, that's not only believable but something we need to get happening really soon! Hand me my gas enriched bananas laced with magic, I'm onto it fellas, it's going to be awesome, it's going to be so cool people will be saying 'check this thingy out, it's unimaginable!'

Wait UN-*IMAGINABLE?* How can someone ever, fucking EVER, describe, or reference something, and then say it's un*imaginable*? Un*imaginable*? Un*IMAGINABLE*??? *ANYTHING IS IMAGINABLE*, you you you YOU BASTARD!' I want to yell AAAAAAAGGAGHHHGHGHHHH!!!!!!

Five

The sad rainbow – a children's book

'I'm sad' said the rainbow, to his only friend, the dried dog poo.

'Are you sad because you only get to come out when it's raining?' the dried dog poo asked.

'No' replied the sad rainbow, 'but now that I think of it, you're right, I never get to come out on a purely sunny day, that does really suck'.

'Are you sad because everyone assumes you're gay?' the dried dog poo asked.

'No' replied the sad rainbow, 'but everyone does always assume I'm gay, just because I'm a rainbow. But that's just a nasty stereotype, and I hate nasty stereotypes'.

'Are you sad because you basically look like a giant frown?' the dried dog poo asked.

'No' replied the sad rainbow 'but I've never even thought about that before, but oh my God you're right, I am the exact shape of a frown. That's awful, oh my God, I am the world's biggest frown'.

'Are you sad because sometimes it's really windy in Sydney, making it difficult for a really cool guy named David Tieck to read the newspaper in the park, or eat cotton candy on a lonely bridge, his two favorite activities?' the dried dog poo asked.

'No' replied the sad rainbow, 'but that really sucks, David Tieck is an awesome guy and he deserves better than that.'

'Are you sad because you can't pick just one color, you have to show off all the time and be like "look at me, I'm EVERY color, that's better than you dried poo, I can't just be brown once in a while cause I have to shooooow off"?' the dried dog poo asked.

'No' replied the sad rainbow, 'But now that you say that, you're right, I always have to be fancy, sometimes a rainbow just wants to relax in jeans and a plain t-shirt too!'

'Are you sad because your only friend is a dried dog poo who's kind of an angry prick who likes to point out all your flaws?' the dried dog poo asked.

'No' replied the sad rainbow, 'but you are being particularly mean today, I was already sad, but now I'm practically mortified, what's your problem?'

'My problem is that I am trying to help you, and you can't just friggin' spit out why you're sad!' Said the dried dog poo, 'For Christ sake I'm sick of always having to guess shit with you! Just say it already!!!!!'

'Well what about you?' retorted the sad rainbow, 'like *you* can talk, you're always like "I'm dry, I smell" you're a freaking whiner!'

'Just tell me why you're sad' pleaded the dried dog poo 'seriously man, the sun will come out and then I won't see you for weeks! Just get to the fucking point!'

'Ok, ok, you're right' apologized the sad rainbow 'I'm sorry'.

'So why are you fucking sad?' the dried dog poo asked.

'Well, it's just, well' began the sad rainbow on what was sure to be the start of a beautiful soliloquy 'I see humans wearing hats all the time, and they always look so cool and hip, but when I visualize wearing a hat I can't even imagine one that might suit me. And I imagine wearing hats *all the time*, whenever I get the chance really, but I have a weird head, and I just don't think hats suit me.'

'Oh my God' exclaimed the dried dog poo, 'You're a rainbow, you can't wear hats you idiot, you're not solid, you're just refracted light, they'd fall straight through you!'

'Screw you!' yelled the sad rainbow 'You'll never understand what it's like to be me'!

Just then a German Shepherd came by and ate the dried dog poo before licking its owners face.

The End

Six

Finally a very important anthropological study

Call me crazy, but I have spent a hell of a lot of time thinking about this, and I have come to the logical conclusion that if an ant climbed to the top of a mountain and immediately yelled:

'I'm the king of the castle and you're a dirty rascal'.

It'd then quickly follow this sentence up with:

'Fuck it was a long way up here, plus what the hell is a dirty rascal?'

I know, it seems so obvious now that I have written it in sentence form, but for many years anthropologists (people who study the ways different people and societies have lived over history, but occasionally get chucked some 'ant study grant money' based on administrative cock ups due to their field's poorly thought out first three letters of their name) have wondered what would happen if an ant ever reached the summit of a mountain, and have failed to figure out anything, due to ants small stature, poor climbing skills, and the size of mountains in regions they inhabit. Also anthropologists waste a hell of a lot of time on the pots ancient people used, and pots are not interesting at all. Consider this list of things more interesting than pots:

- Coffee stains.
- The poorly regulated olive-picking unions.
- Wheelbarrows full of filament.
- Ants, they walk in a line, that's really cool.

Sure of course, if instead of 'mountain' we merely switched in 'ant hill', we would find lots of ants who had climbed to the top, but that is not impressive at all, in fact switch the species to humans and it sounds almost like you are a genocide fan:

'Today I climbed a human hill!'
'Really, you're into genocide? That's so 2003, get away from me you unimpressive loser.'

Yep that's how sad the life of anthropologists and ants are, forever trying to scale the heights of anthropology and/or high things.

And really it's the ants I feel sorry for, because the word 'ant' is merely the word 'an' with another singular letter added. These are very small animals, and that is a very small addition to an already very small word; a word that itself was very mediocre to begin with. So why the hell does an ant deserve to be king of anything, let alone a mountain?

I think ants would be more remarkable if they had have shunted adding the letter 't' to 'an' and instead gone with 'anf' or even more fun 'anh'. How fun would it be pronouncing that all the time? It's almost unpronounceable. And saying almost unpronounceable words is one of the funnest things anyone can ever do. Consider these fun hard to pronounce words:

- Constituents.
- Entrepreneurial.
- Fandangle.
- Hierarchical.
- Obstetrician.
- Flan.

I could spend two or three hours having fun just saying these six words alone, add 'anh' to the mix and there is a fun weekend.

Although it would make it way harder to insult them:

'Hey you, you dirty an.., um, angh, how the hell do I say what you are????'

Before you know it they WOULD be king of stuff, because how the hell do you stop something you can't insult?

There would be NOTHING you could do to stop them, except, well, stepping on them, but is it worth climbing off your human hill to do that? Hmmm is it? Wow, what an intriguing human action that would be. Climbing off a hill made of humans specifically to step on an ant. And the best thing is that it would be totally relatable and relevant to today's humans. Not like stupid pots. This is definitely something the Anthropological society should get working on immediately. Well either that or finding out what the hell IS a dirty rascal?

Seven

A word from a Dictator's son

Pre-essay Warning: I'm taking a break from science and humor for a brief moment to bring you something sad. Please prepare tissues for yourself before even *attempting* to read the forthcoming story.

This is a story I've exclusively acquired. I knew something was up as soon as I saw a man with seventeen slaves forcing one of the few that still had both his hands to write down what he was saying onto several cocktail napkins in a bar I was frequenting one night. I was able to snatch these napkins while this man took one of his slaves outside to have his hand cut off for spilling a beer, and upon reading the notes it turned out this man was the son of a Dictator, and tonight was not his night. This was what was written down on his behalf:

I just walked into this bar precisely as the band ended their set. Honestly I heard the last chord and then the singer seriously immediately said 'we're taking a break'. Assholes. My Heated Jetty business closed down today so I'm really sad. I sunk like a billion dollars into that business and it's all gone! I still don't get it. People love hovercrafts right? But who wants to leave their warm ocean side mansion and walk on a cold jetty to get to their heated hovercraft? I'm right, right? Those two minutes walking in the cold can be almost unbearably a tiny bit irritating! So buy a Heated Jetty, what's the problem? It just makes no sense. I don't know anyone else who sells Heated Jetties, so where are people getting them?

Fuck I hate the West, that's the third one of my businesses that's failed here so far. I barely had a single customer at my Camel Diaper Store, and the Female Circumcision business didn't take off one little bit. People even said it was 'wrong', um, how can stopping women from getting any pleasure from sex be 'wrong?' THEY'RE WOMEN, they DON'T DESERVE PLEASURE!!! Assholes. And what are people doing with their pet camels? Just letting them shit anywhere? People here are disgusting.

They don't like my ideas either. They didn't take to my 'bring your lion to your friend's amusement park day' idea. And they never even listened when I told the local fire fighters they'd have more work if they used bazookas on retirement villages.

I'm down to my last three billion in allowance now, if I don't turn things around soon I'm going to have to ask dad to take over yet another country, and you have no idea how hard those calls are to make, there are like so many international phone codes, it takes up like ten minutes to dial them all, it's the worst, you just can not imagine, seriously. I shouldn't have to live like this.

I can't believe Pops sent me here to Oklahoma. 'Get to know the enemy' he said 'learn to live on your own'. Fuck you Pops, your dad never made you 'get to know the enemy'. And you got to start shooting children in the face when you were twelve, but you made me wait till I was fourteen, just to be superior. You asshole.

I just wanted to hear some music playing tonight but the band said they were going on a break. Couldn't they have their slaves play in their absence? If those were my slaves I'd have cut off one of their body parts for making me look this bad.

Who am I kidding?' I'd cut up their bodies regardless! Ha ha, at least I haven't lost my sense of humor yet! Oh man, I'm not even allowed to call them 'my slaves' here. The people here say they 'regret' the period in their history when they had slaves, what the hell is wrong with people? Anyway I've had a few drinks here, and the band hasn't restarted, there are no cute skinny Muslim virgins here, and my onion rings are taking forever! I'm just not in a good mood. I might just go home and snuggle up in bed with my lion, or maybe I'll go find a twelve year old to rape, I might even be nice and wait till AFTER to circumcise her. Ha ha, yep the sense of humor is still strong, yay.

That's the end of what was written on those cocktail napkins, but the Dictator's son's story didn't end there. Asmid got run over by a drunk driver later that night while stumbling back to his house and died a long painful death in a pile of dirty snow next to a dead skunk that had been run over a few weeks earlier. Still reading his story is sad isn't it? Hard to take really. I mean because he was damn right, international phone codes *are* still hard to use and very annoying to people! I mean my God, when will the world learn. When damn it, when?

Eight

Don't dump your trash here

What a tool that Dictator's son was, um, *real* men walk down their jetty to their hovercrafts wearing a bevy of naked ladies, you tool. Oh man, I would love to write an angry story about that guy, but to be honest, I'm too busy being jealous of trash.

And yes I'm not stupid, I know how controversial revealing this in a public forum may turn out to be. I am well aware that some people can regularly be heard saying 'don't make me jealous of the trash', I know that there are signs up around town like 'don't feed the trash' and 'it's dangerous to both man and trash if trash learns to see humans as a source of food' and I know that current affair shows do reports on how some trash is actually undercover fabric salesmen doing their 'research' as they call it (call it what it is *fabric salesmen* - you lying trash - it's being a busy body! And I have had a busy body in my bed once and I was all like 'stay still' and she was like 'I prefer to get busy' and I was all 'that isn't going to contribute to a fully relaxing sleeping environment' and then she got all mad and left and went home! That's right, 'busy bodies' mean 'belligerent bodies'!)

The point is I am not an idiot, I know most people are scared of trash, and it seems like they have perfectly logical and valid reasons to be scared, and I don't want to disregard that, but I simply don't agree with these frightened folk, because if you really think about it, trash has the best fucking life ever. Yes it's true. Because as trash, its life's work is complete! It was designed to hold something before a human used it and that has now happened!!!!!

Wow, it's like history right in front of us. You can walk past and be all like 'hey Billy, see that candy bar wrapper, that once had candy in it!!!' And Billy can be like 'Hey dad, this strange man is offering me candy'! That's the genius of trash! (Please note: This works best if you're near a kid named Billy and his father, if Billy's dad isn't around its just creepy).

But that's not why I am jealous of it. No, it's the fact that with it's life's work now complete it has nothing at all left to do but lay out in the sun, day after day, soaking up the rays, watching the world go by, and letting drunk teenagers urinate on it, it's all the joy of old age without any of the lack of joy of old age! Wow, that's awesomely paradoxical.

Oh, trash
Oh, trash
That's the life for me
Living life with glee
Oh, trash
Oh, trash
Laying out fancy-free
Wait who's that pissing on me?

That is not yet the theme song of trash, but if they ever develop the ability to sing then it damn well should be. You know, assuming it turns out they speak with Shakespearean like eloquence, and become all snotty so they decide to talk about themselves as like a product rather than in the first person. I mean humans don't sing 'oh, human, oh, human' so get off your 'pretentious stagecoach' trash.

Wait, um, I mean I'm jealous of trash. Trash by definition is in retirement, and sometimes it reaches this career milestone mere days after it was given birth to, and sometimes it's made of substances guaranteeing that it will live for thousands of years! Can you imagine, knowing that you'll live for thousands of years and still getting to retire three days after birth? No you can't, because you ain't trash. Jealous? I am! But wait, maybe you *shouldn't* be. 'Why'? I hear you ask? 'You've just made it clear to us that trash has THE life?'

I'll tell you why!

Because there are these sadistic bastards who call themselves things like 'cleaners', 'trash pickeruperers' and 'seriously guys, I don't mean to whine but some people and their trash is so gross, I guess I'll just pick it up because I am better than themerers' who go around town, picking up these pieces of trash, while they are innocently chilling out in the sun enjoying their hard earned post career relaxing years, and these people often throw these poor pieces of trash in plastic bags and suffocate them to death!

Wow, can you even contemplate what it must be like to suddenly be chucked in a plastic bag and cut off from air? It would be terrible. But even worse than that, trash has no arms or legs to fight off its attackers, or try to break free of the plastic, it just has to lie there, feel the oxygen disappear, and then wait for the pain to get so overwhelming it passes out right before death (horrifically pieces of trash often shit their pants right before they die from suffocating, although they prefer that this information doesn't get out to the greater public).

What kind of a world do we live in when this sort of brutal behaviour goes not merely unpunished, but sometimes even celebrated? Sometimes people have 'murder trash parties' (or as they call them 'can someone stay after the party and help clean up the trash?') sometimes criminals as part of jail work release programs are forced into trash murdering! I am sorry, but committing a heinous act does not make up for a life of crime, not in my 'oh, human, oh life, oh existence!'

Sure from time to time some more kind hearted evil trash murderers will at least have the decency to spike the piece of trash to death with a nail on a stick to save it from being suffocated, yet still often those nails are rusty, and most people don't know this, but tetanus is amazingly swift forming in trash, and is often as painful as suffocating to death.

And anyway, their bodies are still inhumanely, sorry I mean intrashely crushed together in huge compactors often alongside other corpses of trash that are not just not family, but sometimes even whole different species! If you crush a human body, a dog body, and an old rug together in a compactor then there is an outcry (let we not forget the great human/dog/rug tragedy of 1913, or 'huogug' as it was called by the tabloids at the time, ha ha, tabloids are so adorable), yet crush a soda can, a shoe box, and a discarded pair of broken sunglass frames together and no one even raises an eyebrow (please note: Some people are not capable of raising just one eyebrow, but if they could most would still not raise one about this monstrosity!)

I know; it's disgusting!

Then to compound the calamity they are then buried, often naked, in mass unmarked graves know as 'landfills' (um they're filled with trash corpses not 'land'), which are then turned into parks where children are encouraged to play on their graves!!!!!!

Seriously - '!!!!!' - I know it's excessive exclamation pointing, but kids playing on mass unmarked graves, well honestly - '!!!!!!!'

I know you'll get some 'realists' who claim that retired containers, and even things like receipts from products long since consumed are 'no longer contributing to society'. Well first off I have to say – maybe YOU'RE not contributing to society! (You probably are, I mean you're saying stuff out loud that's contributing something, but I just wanted you to know how it felt to be accused of perhaps not contributing to society – it's soft isn't it? Which is surprising at first because most people don't know that 'society' uses softener) but that doesn't change the UNDENIABLE fact that trash serves a VALUABLE purpose in society!

Don't believe me? Well cop this truth. Say you're walking through a neighbourhood, rather like the one where I was staying when I had these trash inspired awakening epiphanies (Korea Town, Los Angeles), and you will encounter a large array of both discarded condom wrappers and heroin needles. Yep, you get to know right off the bat that the kids around here are both scared of STDs and equally fearless of STDs, a contrast which screams 'these kids play by their own rules'. This kind of information is priceless when a street football game breaks out and you're asked to play, because you don't have to say 'hey kids, what rules do you play by' because you already *know*, they play by their *own* rules. That saves you the entire length of time that this exchange would have taken, and time is invaluable, especially if, like me, you're prone to daydreaming about how to ban all electric drills from kindergartens. Yep:

Trash: 1
Realists: 0
Hell Yeah.

Oh by the way, if you do get involved in this game of football and one of the kids bleeds, you also know not to taste the blood for signs of a bizarre chocolate flavor, because heroin boys? Really? Heroin boys? Awwww, I hate to feel this way, but I'm disappointed in you. And I am afraid I have to punish you, I know I am sorry, but heroin boys? Really? I am sorry, I can't give you dessert after dinner tonight, and tonight is chocolate cheesecake night. No, no, no, you MADE me do that, I don't feel one little tiny bit good about it, but heroin boys? Really? Boo.

Oh, check this out – go to a neighbourhood full of fast food wrapper trash and you can reliably conclude that this is a fat neighbourhood, which means a slow neighbourhood, and therefore a muggers paradise! That's VALUABLE information for muggers.

Note: Sometimes something valuable to individuals is damaging to society as a whole.

Note 2: Don't you dare blame trash for that – it doesn't CHOOSE where it is dumped, it merely offers you the precious ability to read a neighbourhood for what it is, so don't go 'we don't want muggers coming here' instead be all like 'thanks trash for letting us know the TRUTH about what's going on in the streets, unlike those street glorifying hip-hop singers'.

Note 3: Remember when 'hip-hop' used to be called 'rap'? Did they change the name to try and make us forget that one time those rappers did that one thing, you know, that bad thing? Cause I for one will NEVER forget!

Note 4: Do something nice for the world, collect a bunch of fast food wrappers and dump them in a neighbourhood full of fit people, the muggers will never know what hit them, and really don't you owe this to trash?

Note 5: Heroin boys? Really? Boo.

Nine

I'd still go

True story: One day recently, something *amazing* happened to me - I just randomly, out of the blue, with no clue it could even be possible, discovered amongst the trash heap that is my bedroom floor - a French coin to the value of five Francs.

Do you know what that means? I now own five French Francs! Yay.

But also, even more obviously, because the French have not used the delightful Franc since switching to the Euro over a decade or so ago, that this means that a French Person, who probably doesn't empty out his pockets anywhere near often enough, must have once, probably over a decade ago, snuck into my bedroom and performed some sort of an act which caused this coin to dislodge itself from his pocket, and then he decided that rather than put said coin back in his pocket, he would instead hide it in a place so hidden that it remained unfound for about a decade, and then all that time later he snuck back into my bedroom and removed it from its hiding place and instead of returning it to his pocket, he just left in in the middle of my floor!

Wow.

I'm guessing that he must have done some sit-ups maybe, or he was so excited to find a pair of my used underpants that he jumped for joy, or perhaps he suddenly got a weird feeling that the world should be upside down and that he should be walking on the ceilings. (True story: as a kid I spent hours lying on my back, staring at the ceiling, and pretending the world was upside down, I don't know how I then grew up to be so normal). I really don't care. However it got there, it's a super exciting mystery for me to enjoy. A mystery with a character who is probably French. It's very exciting. Seriously.

Here is where the excitement really takes off though - if there is another World War and France get kicked out of the European Union for surrendering too fast and are therefore forced to give up the Euro and revert back to their previous currency, and make an interesting choice to set it's value to be the same as it was in 1979, and I find myself in France sometime after that, then I can totally buy a croissant with those Five French Francs. YEEEESSSS!!!

Now I know what you're thinking - why would you buy a regular croissant when you could just as easily buy a *chocolate* croissant? And you're right. A chocolate croissant is *way* more delicious than a regular croissant, and those do not require an additional expense for butter or some form of jam, or perhaps even some cheese, but let's be realistic here for a second - there is *no way* that the European Union is going to go to the extreme lengths of kicking France out, but then still allow them to make chocolate croissants. They are seriously delicious. *Seriously.* Especially in the morning when you get the fresh ones still warm from the oven. Seriously delicious. Yum. Seriously. Or if you chuck them in the microwave you can get them all melty inside. It's seriously delicious. I mean *seriously.* So don't be stupid, as *if* they are going to let them still have those? Just no fucking way. The truth is this:

'After a unanimous vote of all remaining European Union countries we have declared that only holding out Germany for three weeks really was seriously pathetic, so France that's it, you're out. Go on, get on out of here. Get. France, don't make me hit you with a rolled up newspaper……. Oh by the way, also, you can't make chocolate croissants anymore, they're too seriously delicious, now get'.

Truth be told if this was all going down they would probably ban them doing a whole bunch of things. And for the record I can now exclusively report the entire list of things that will get banned in France if there is a third World War and France gets kicked out of the European Union for surrendering too fast. Sourced exclusively from my own personal suggestions. Some of these may seem harsh, just like with the no more chocolate croissants, but if they're not punished they'll never learn. Here is the list:

1. French people will no longer be allowed to put paper into recycling bins, it's too prejudice against other forms of trash, and trash, as I have proven, is an awesome thing, and as *if* prejudice against awesome things will be allowed.
2. French people will no longer be allowed to watch a surprising yet inspirational speech and respond with a silent pause, followed by a slow clap. (They *will be* allowed to write 'slow clap' on a piece of paper and slyly hand it to a police officer).
3. French people will no longer be allowed to listen to any songs recorded by Elton John between 1978-1982 (that one is just obvious).
4. If any French person gets injured in a football match the said injured player will no longer be allowed to 'walk it off'.
5. If a French person gets a stomach-ache from eating too many chocolate croissants they *also* can't 'walk it off' because they'd be lying! Because obviously chocolate croissants are BANNED, seriously banned!

I know these are all very tough punishments. And some of you are no doubt thinking I am cruel for suggesting them, especially as I used the word 'official' somewhere near that list (possibly) and that is a very authoritive word, so it's pretty much all guaranteed to happen now. So sorry. But remember, I have already volunteered to go back to France, even in their new harsh world. Because I love France; and I have Five French Francs to spend. Also, ironically (possibly) I found these particular Francs right before this catastrophic turn of events began, that's got to be fate or something. So I'll still go. Unless it turns out the intruder who dropped the Francs WAS doing sit-ups, you French dudes exercise and still only held out three weeks? Pathetic. Seriously Pathetic.

Ten

Who wants an awesome job?

If someone ever randomly asked me if I wanted to control the tollbooth levies I think twelve very distinct and important questions would have to be answered first:

1. Really, me?
2. The tollbooth levies?
3. Control?
4. Do the tollbooths themselves have levies, or is it the levies the tollbooths charge that you want me to control?
5. Control is such a Fascist word; can I just give them guidance?
6. Can I paint them purple?
7. Are people really 'born' gay?
8. What *is* the big deal with misusing the words 'their', 'there' and 'they're'? All these Fascists just want to complain about anything these days.
9. Why not the bowl tooth levies?
10. My knowledge of the economics surrounding tollbooth levy control is only somewhere in-between intermediate advanced and advanced expert, so really, me?
11. Are you going to answer any of these or should I just keep going?
12. The tollbooth levies?

If the answers came back as:

1. Yes.
2. Yes.
3. No - see later answer.
4. Are you an idiot of course what they charge!
5. I don't think you can be Fascist with a booth.
6. Yes please – we've actually long considered painting over the Swastikas.
7. Yes, sort of, maybe - it's hard to explain DON'T YOU JUDGE ME!
8. Some people's lives are so perfect they have time to concern themselves with trivial bullshit.
9. Because of time wasted on trivial bullshit we're now forced to live in a world so bland bowl tooth levies barely even exist anymore.
10. We would like someone with a bit better credentials but no one else is willing to take this shitty job.
11. Yes I just did.
12. Yeah, why not, it's an awesome job that almost everyone will be fighting over.

Well then yeah, I'd consider taking control of the tollbooth levies, apparently it's an awesome job that almost everyone will be fighting over, so that sounds cool, so you know what, count me in, just as long as there planning on driving me they're otherwise I'd never even consider working their.

Eleven

Ruining it for all the ladies

Girls, now I'm a sensitive, witty, suave, sweet and creative, modern male, so I know that you all hope to never, ever meet me, and instead hope to one day be swept off your feet - by a Knight in shining armour. And as a bitter, jealous, hurt, vindictive, and shallow, modern male, it is now my duty to do all I can to ruin this fantasy for you. Thankfully, as you will soon see, for me this is an easy thing to pull off. Hey some jobs suck; like being a fluffer at a cow breeding ranch or being a heart surgeon (eew blood!), and some are fun; like controlling the tollbooth levies, or ruining every girl on earth's ultimate fantasy. So here goes:

Um, so like, haven't you like ever wondered just why these Knights in 'shining' armour were so concerned with buffing up their suits to a pretty shiny shine, before like heading off to war, where they are destined to see little other than a bunch of men on a battle field being hacked to death with medieval weaponry?

'We're blissfully naive and oblivious to what you're talking about' I hear you say. Ok, well then lets look at some facts about Knights:

- They were christened 'Sir' as in Servant to the Queen, which was also the name of a band headed by a man with a really cool moustache!
- No one ever says 'my grand daddy was a Knight'.

- They rode 'stallions' which are like horses but extra manly and yet have waxed pubes.
- They used 'phallic' weapons like swords, jousts and cannons when they could so easily have just used magic.
- They used a silent 'K', which rhymes with 'gay', a word that now mostly means 'lame', but used to refer to happiness and joy, and Knights spent most of their time joyfully hanging with other men!
- They famously used the battle cry 'whoever cuts off the most heads today gets blown by me tonight, ooh ahhh' that some people think may for some reason have referenced oral sex (for the record 'sucking' is WAY better than 'blowing' in that department). Climate change enthusiasts also use this battle cry as evidence that the world was 'windier' in the Middle Ages.
- They were enthusiastic proponents of the punishment known as being 'drawn and quartered' that referred to being sketched naked with crayons and yet having your 'penis' sketched at only a quarter of it's true size, and back then men were simple and shallow, and didn't want others to think they had small penises, why? Maybe it would mean fewer guys would want to see their penises perhaps? Proving they *did* want men to look at their penises.
- They were called 'Knights' but mostly fought in the 'day' leaving their 'torches' for each other.

That's right, the evidence is all in, and girls I'm sorry but it is agonizingly clear, the dream boat you dream of known collectively as the Knights in shining armour were *clearly*, as I have proven beyond a reasonable doubt, trying to overcompensate for some sort of body odour problem, hoping if they look shiny on the outside people will assume that wretched smell is all the hacked up corpses everywhere, rather than the lack of the invention of deodorant. Sorry, fantasy ruined, those Knights stink. Also 'swept off your feet' – um, didn't you hear, apparently it was way windier in the middle ages, that's what was sweeping ladies off their feet. In conclusion, now that I have ruined all your fantasies, I would like you to instead consider looking for a generous, adventurous, sexy, expressive, and bighearted modern male, like a writer perhaps, that or maybe some sort of giant freak bird, got to be better than a gay Knight.

Twelve

Vicious, Vicious Criminal

If I ever go to jail I want it to be for something really cool…. like vagrancy! Oh man, that would be super awesome. I mean consider this dramatization of what I assume would be an extremely accurate portrayal of my first day in the big house:

Other vicious criminal – 'Hey new guy, whatcha in for?'

Me, only with a cool gruff vicious criminal voice – 'Nothing! And I mean LITERALLY nothing, I'm in jail for doing nothing for *so long* they put me in here, I do my nothing hard, yeah that's right, I nothing to the God damn core. When I'm feeling the demon in my soul I go out somewhere in public and just do nothing for so long and hard the cops are like 'if this guy keeps up with all that nothing he might fucking kill someone, or even eventually be noticed'. That's how bitching my nothing is motherfuckers. So stay away from my toothbrush or I'll nothing you to death!'

Other vicious criminal, only now with a quivering scared voice – 'Oh yeah, I stabbed 32 women to death, mostly for my own sexual satisfaction, I ain't scared of you!'

Me, with my cool gruff vicious criminal voice now more satisfactorily warmed up, and less scratchy after trying it out with my earlier threats to the other vicious criminal and also now full

of the pride and power of knowing I have a big man on campus suddenly quaking in his boots – 'You ain't?'

Other vicious criminal, quivering voice being paralleled with a trembling 'I'm about to cry' chin – 'Nah I ain't'.

Me, gruff, warmed up, prideful and powerful voice getting uncomfortably but controllably loud to really sting the point home – 'You ain't?'

Other vicious criminal, now dead set balling, tears streaming down his face, dripping all over his onesy – 'Nah I ain't'.

Me, gruff, pride, loud, barbed, stinging voice, now also with a chuckle – 'well you should be.'

Chorus of other less vicious criminals now watching, entranced with my power – 'Ooooohhh'

Other vicious criminal, now lying in the foetal position – 'Well I ain't, someone call my mommy please.'

Me, laughing my ass off – 'Well you should be.'

Him – 'well I ain't'.

Me – 'Well you should be'.

Him – 'well I ain't'.

Me – 'well you should be'.

Him, now struggling for air as his prison cell fills up with scared little baby tears – 'prove it'.

A few days later:

Priest, with anger in his eyes and a trembling doubt in his own faith – 'We are gathered here today to remember the life of Tom, an other vicious criminal, cruelly taken so young after David Tieck did nothing so long people started dying. (Now really crying) why didn't the officials stop this before it was too late, who would let a God damn vagrant into our jails? Make that man do *something* for fucks sake'!

Yeah that's right, if I ever go to jail it will be for something VERY cool. Actually the very cool thing about going to jail for vagrancy is the punishment is to continue to do nothing. Jail is literally like a perfect crafted school where people can master vagrancy while being trained and supported by the very people who will one day once again try to punish their vagrancy with more vagrancy! It's like one of those paintings where the stairs go in a circle and appear to always go up, but more like those stairs mixed with a school like Harvard, for a wanna-be criminal man. Wow, the three pillars of cool: jail, stairs and Harvard. I think I may have *actually* talked myself into wanting to become a vagrant. I would do it too, but I'm just too viciously lazy, but still, stay away from my fucking toothbrush!

Thirteen

Please don't watch (re-watch) *The Titanic* until you read this

One movie that many, many people have seen, or even heard about, is one called *The Titanic*, about a boat called *The Titanic*. Although you may not have seen this movie, and I don't want to assume you have because, true story, I once saw a man eating a hamburger with chopsticks! And despite this act being unbelievably interesting almost no one I have spoken to has even heard about it, let alone seen it. That's why I don't do assumptions on people's entertainment knowledge.

I may be in the minority here, but I say this is proof that real life is sometimes in fact *more* interesting than fiction. And it's in this spirit, that I've decided to finally reveal a very, very dark, real life, true family secret.

My Great, Great Grandfather, Harvey, was ON the Titanic! (This isn't the secret by the way, but still too cool to not warrant a dramatic one-line announcement that could only possibly be spoiled by an inclusion of unnecessary explanation following the big reveal!)

And here is the secret - one night, during the famed maiden voyage, Harvey was on deck going for a stroll when a man came up to him hurriedly and said 'hey, it's Harvey right? You have a car on the ship don't you? Well a couple of filthy kids just fucked in it and left gross sweaty hand prints all over it!'

In a rage my Great, Great Grandfather Harvey ran to his car and what he saw there made him go 'eeeewwwwww'. Sure enough, there *were* gross sweaty handprints on the windows, and all sorts of bodily fluids on the back seat, and one of those bodily fluids was splooge, and splooge is the ickiest of all bodily fluids.

'You don't fuck in someone else's car, you just don't!' Harvey yelled. 'eeeewwwwww' he added.

Later, during this very same voyage, and you may or may not know this, so spoiler alert, but the Titanic sank. Still, despite the horror of the iceberg, lack of lifeboats, dead frozen bodies all around, including the body of a lady that Harvey had seen once and hoped to talk to eventually but never got the chance, there really was one thing about the whole ordeal that stuck with him: Harvey just could not get the idea that people had fucked in his car out of his mind, even after the miracle of his survival (he shared a piece of drift wood, only cunts don't share).

He did everything he could to get the grossness out of his mind. He even sent a recovery crew to the sink sight to recover his car just so he could burn it.

'You don't fuck in someone else's car, you just don't!' Harvey yelled as the car burned 'eeeewwwwww' he added, but it wasn't enough.

This became the obsession of his life. Trying to stop people fucking in stranger's cars became his life's work. He would tell anyone he met anywhere. Friends and strangers alike. He even took a job as a car salesman for a while, he figured anytime he could sell a car to someone it would allow them to fuck in their own cars instead of other people's.

'Can I interest you in a new Ford' Harvey would say to prospective customers 'I hope so, because you don't fuck in someone else's car, you just don't!' he would continue, 'eeeewwwwww' he'd add as they walked away.

After he was fired from that job for some reason, he just began ranting on the street, ranting at church and even ranting on corporate golf retreats. One time he was in a golf foursome with some associates when one asked about his refusal to ride in the golf cart.

'You don't fuck in someone else's car, you just don't!' Harvey told them while he looked at the cart, 'eeeewwwwww' he added, noting that none of his colleagues owned their particular golf carts and yet all three were currently fucking in them.

Well one of those colleges was quite taken aback by my Great, Great Grandfather Harvey's attitude, taken really super far aback. You see he was a man who regularly fucked in other people's cars, only he'd never thought about how gross it might be. 'Maybe it's because of the splooge I always leave behind' he suddenly thought.

That mans name was Gerald Durex. He went on to invent the condom, at the time specifically so he could fuck in other peoples cars without leaving splooge behind, but ultimately turning the condom into the invention that would render just about all casual sex into an act that feels far less good than it could, whether in your own car, or God forbid, someone else's.

In fact condom use has now become so rife that I have heard that some people are so detached from physical contact they even use chopsticks to eat hamburgers! And it's all my Great, Great Grandfather Harvey's fault.

Well I guess this is all pretty much public knowledge now, however I should also point out my Great, Great Grand Father Harvey actually *died* on the Titanic! Yep, saying he survived above was just a lie. Harvey was sadly standing by his car when the iceberg hit.

'You don't fuck in someone else's car, you just don't!' he was yelling as The Titanic hit the iceberg, 'eeeewwwwww' he added as water filled up this section of the underbelly of the boat drowning him.

And no one even *tried* to swim down, drag his body out, give him mouth to mouth until he began breathing again, and then share a piece of drift wood with him, those non-sharing cunts.

That's right, everything that happened since, the car burning, the car selling job, the golf retreats, the numb casual sex, all happened with his ghost! He's sitting behind me watching me type this as we speak.

So there it is, my family's big dark secret. That my friends, is *real* life. So please don't watch (re-watch) a movie about a gold digger who cheats on her fiancé with a dreamy third classer with awesomely realistic special affects, clearly real life is way more interesting than fiction.

But if you do watch it, despite my warnings, please keep your ears open during the scene when they fuck in that stranger's car, if you listen closely you may be able to hear the ghost of my Great, Great Grandfather Harvey whispering gently in your ear.

'You don't fuck in someone else's car, you just don't!' he'll whisper, and if you're lucky he might just add 'eeeewwwwww'.

Fourteen

Don't wash your pants until you check the pockets for heaven

One thing I have always loved about my Great, Great Grandfather Harvey is that his regular presence in my life has proven to me beyond a shadow of a doubt that there is a very real and accessible after life. Which was why when I recently saw a sign outside of a church, it really made me think. This sign proclaimed:

THERE'S A LOT OF HEAVEN CRAMMED ONTO EARTH

That is, awesome! Because that essentially means that one of the Angles went up to God one day and they had the following exchange:

God - (Pick your own God like voice, I personally prefer to ignore the traditional deep and manly and go for a good solid effeminate young Danish boy). You wanted to see me Angel? Come on in.

Angel – (Deep and manly, Australian accent, obviously) Hey God mate, um, so I wanted to raise something with you, um, thing is there really is a hell of a lot of heaven up here in heaven, I mean practically everything in heaven is heaven; it's a God damn administrative nightmare!

God - Sorry man, I know, I never expected so many people to end up, up here, geez so many people are just so darn good, barely a bad thing could be said about any of them, so we have expanded a lot. Tell you what, why don't just cram a lot of heaven onto earth?

Angel – um, Earth really? Not Randlton in south east of universe 179, they're really crying out for some heaven. Or maybe Lievendtonalvle in the deep blunder of Universe 745, they don't even have Internet porn yet; we could give them some heaven?

God – Ugh, um, maybe don't question my wisdom Angel, I am fucking God!

Angel – Yes, yes I'm sorry.

God - Besides Randleton didn't kill the son I sent them like I told them too, they made him a celebrity instead, can you imagine, a self centered everything come easy pretentious celebrity? Do you know what a brat he is now? I'm having a hell of a time trying to get him to clean his room.

Angel - Sir you're God, why don't you hire a cleaner, I'm sure we can find you a Romanian lady, or maybe a Taiwanese lady, or possibly even a Bangladeshi man?

God - It's about discipline! It's about fucking respect! You can't let your kids think just cause they're Son of God everything comes easy.

Angel – I'm sorry. You're right God.

God – I'm right? Thanks so much, your support and understanding means a tremendous lot to me, without it I just don't know how I would handle the doubt? *Seriously where do I find these idiots?* I'm FUCKING GOD you tool, OF COURSE I AM RIGHT!

Angel – Sorry, sorry, yes of course, um, well just one more thing I guess, when you say 'cram' some heaven onto earth, are you sure we don't wish to be more careful and perhaps gently place a bit of heaven, isn't cramming a bit of a haphazard way to distribute stuff?

God - Oh my God you are a nuisance aren't you, just stuff a pile of it into the vortex and stick your foot in and cram it in good and deep, for fuck's sake.

Angel – But, but it'll wrinkle!

God – Holy shit, it's fucking heaven! It doesn't matter where it goes, how much it wrinkles, it's fucking HEAVEN! They'll deal with it. You know what, I bet they'll even put up a sign somewhere to commemorate it.

Angel – You really think so? A sign? Where, like a billboard or something?

God – I reckon probably outside a church somewhere.

Angel – Wow, now THAT would be cool. But I just can't see it happening if it's all crammed and wrinkled?

God – Tell you what, if I am right you pay for my internet porn for a month, if you are right I'll pay for yours.

Angel – You're on, it's a bet!

God – (walking away, under breath) What a moron, I'M fucking GOD! Of course I am fucking right. Anyway, Hell fucking Yeah, free Internet porn for a month, suck on that Lievendtonalvle!

Fifteen

Exclusive: How the entire world is in danger!

This is a matter of critical importance, the entire world and all of its peoples, animals, minerals and even wrinkled heaven bits are at immediate risk!

Ok, so, here is something I have observed, and if you ask me observation is now one of the most reliable ways of noticing things, so this shit is definitely real, get ready for a bombshell people - often times when I go to use a public toilet I discover that the previous occupier has left the toilet un-flushed, and YET, when I go to use the flush it works fine! OH MY GOD.

Clearly this means that in the time between the previous user and myself using this particular toilet the flush mechanism has SELF-REPAIRED itself! If this wasn't such a God damn serious story, I might even say 'self-repairs itself silly'.

But this IS a serious bit of serious journalism because it get's worse, get ready to have shrapnel rip apart your flesh people - sometimes this remarkable ability to self-repair, or heal, can be performed in seconds! Yes, sometimes a man (or a woman, because I'm not sexist, which means I'm allowed to use any toilet I want) will exit the toilet cubicle just as I am about to enter, and in the mere time it has taken for us to switch places the flush mechanism will now look, act and perform as if it was never even injured, let alone not working at all! Oh my God, this is definitely a definite serious observation now, get ready for your skin grafts and burnt flesh smell covering cologne people – I think if people realized what was *actually* going on here that even the silliest scallywag may sit up and go, 'OH MY GOD'.

Some important questions must be asked here:

1. How come people often use the term 'bombshell' but then choose not to follow on with the beautiful imagery that is gifted with the metaphor?
2. Self-repair? What on earth has the ability to self-repair? And
3. Why doesn't my home toilet ever self-repair when broken?

The alarming answers are alarmingly as follows:

1. Because they are gutless, like for example perhaps a bombshell has exploded near them and ripped apart their entire lower torso, spilling out all their guts in a way that they can no longer claim to own them, rendering them gutless.
2. Living things! That's what. And
3. Clearly your home toilets are different from public ones!

That's right, based on this irrefutable evidence public toilets are obviously living things!

And worse, seeing as no such known living animals or plants on earth have any attributes like these toilets; hard porcelain mouths, thirst for water, rapid healing speeds or ability to mimic common household toilets, then they must be alien!

DID YOU HEAR ME? ALIENS. HERE ON EARTH. THAT YOU EXPOSE YOUR GENITALIA TO!

And these aren't your average, normal, evil, yet stupid run of the mill aliens that we are all used to, like computer stealing crack addicts, Rugby League fans, and people who see girls wearing tank tops with no bra and don't try and think of an excuse for them to bend and twist, no these aliens are highly intelligent, able to infiltrate public bathrooms around the world, and manipulate commercial building managers into thinking they have ordered and installed regular toilets.

That's not all, these aliens have managed to tap into the human psyche, allowing the cynical among us to contemplate the existence of fellow humans who are so lazy and disgusting that instead of flushing a toilet they have just used they instead think their fellow man should have to look and smell their urine and feces! Good God.

'Fuck you aliens! I would NEVER think my fellow man could be that lazy and disgusting!' is what we should all be screaming. But sadly I think some people actually DO believe such lazy disgusting humans may exist. Well open your eyes people.

Consider this - sometimes you will find a toilet seat covered in urine - clear PROOF that the previous user of the toilet found the toilet seat locked into the down position. Obviously. Only thing is that when you test this out, the toilet seat now lifts easily! Obviously this is an amazingly remarkable alien skill in itself, but it comes with the added psychological bent of not merely pitting man vs. man, but man vs. woman. Sometimes even affecting relationships!

Well I for one will not just stand idly by waiting for the people of earth to become so occupied with alien manipulated infighting that the aliens can launch a sneak all out assault!

I say call the cops, get the FBI on this, the X-file people, Scotland Yard, Interpol, the Marines, The Green Berets, The Mafia, the Yemenis Gorilla Militia, sexy girls in tank tops with no bras, the Navy or anyone you know, and next time *you* encounter one of these 'broken' toilets, don't just leave your piss and shit for me to discover - come out and let everyone know THAT'S NOT A TOILET IT'S AN ALIEN - RUN FOR YOUR LIVES!

I am sorry to have to fill you with such fear, but these aliens are camped around the world, concentrating mostly in well built up regions, shopping malls, public park toilets, office bathrooms, and other places with frequently used toilets, while they seemingly almost ignore rural regions (except truck stops). Their plan must be to hit the cities, yet still, please don't worry too much, for I believe I have spotted a weakness.

In my personal toilet use, which is quite frequent as I consume enormous amounts of beverages of all kind, and also I have a shy bladder when it comes to urinals, so I always use the stalls, and yet I encounter an alien toilet, filled with unflushed urine and/or feces, that has self-repaired itself since its last user approximately 93% of the time I need to go. A huge percentage. Yet…

I personally almost NEVER encounter a toilet CURRENTLY in the broken flush or locked seat positions, at most, maybe 0.000001% of the time. This is an astronomical anomaly.

Based on my experiences I can confidently say that clearly the leader of the aliens has sent a direct order - 'if you suspect the human is suspicious then act normal.'

So I say spread the word. Act suspicious. If you encounter a toilet that doesn't seem to have a lifting seat or working flush, don't just leave your filth behind for the next person to find, talk to it. Yelling 'I'm on to you, you alien beast, self-repair now or I'll kick you' might work. Or try taking a photo of it and posting it on social media sites with the caption 'look what the aliens made me do'. Maybe the toilet will self-repair right away and you can flush, something I am positive ALL my fellow humans would do anytime it is humanly possible. Or maybe they won't, but your fellow humans will see your internet posts and immediately give you respect for trying.

If everyone gets on board there may still be hope for the human race! And only then can we perhaps start to take the time to learn from the aliens, and perhaps steal their self-repair skills for ourselves to be used for good – like, you know, with something vital, like fixing broken vending machines. I mean sometimes I just want a beverage something silly and I can't get one, and that's just the sort of problem that may become critical one day, it may even be worth dropping some bombshells, perhaps even dropping bombshells something silly. With the metaphor followed to charred bodies? You bet your ass.

Sixteen

My morning so far

I woke up on the right side of the bed, but my bed was on the wrong side of the room, and my walls had been wallpapered with images of leaves, as it turns out the sleep walking version of me is an interior decorator! This scared me for a moment until I realised it's better to be a sleep walking decorator than being a sleep walking genital mutilator, and that cheered me up so I got out of bed.

I made the bed, because I am a sucker for useless chores, and then I got dressed, because I am a sucker for useless chores, and I went outside where there was a man on the street eating a bowl of cornflakes. I said 'hey man don't you know cornflakes were originally designed to curtail masturbation?' and he replied 'Well do you see me masturbating?' and I looked down at him and realized this guy had three arms, and with his third arm you're God damn right he was jerking it, so I said a jealous 'touché' and shook his hand and I walked away.

Up the street I ran into a kitten and a puppy but I wasn't sure if the noise I made was an awww or an eeewww, because the kitten was pooping on a sunflower and the puppy was urinating on a teddy bear, so I said sort of aaaweeawwwaeeewwaa and walked away so confused I had to stop for a hot dog wrapped in pizza, now my pants feel tight, thanks a fucking lot kitten and puppy.

Suddenly I was abducted by a scientist who shrunk me to a miniature size and injected me into a mans bladder allowing me a magical journey out of his penis, it sure was a lot of fun but when the scientist brought me back to full size and I complained that she hooked me up with a

52

penis and not a vagina the scientist got angry and she said 'women don't urinate out of their vaginas, it comes out there urethra you fool' I said 'hmmm I feel like LICKING your urethra' and then she kicked me out for some reason.

I was so upset that I was cornered into coming up with the following names for my new band (that I have been trying to start for about six years, I'm still the only member, maybe the problem is me?)

- Craving and Enslaving.
- Desperate Delusion Face.
- Simply People not Monkeys, People damn it.
- Naively Unaware Trash Can Lids.
- Blissfully Insane Blankets.
- The Lives We Touched (not in a paedophile way).
- A Last Time Together as Friends (assuming I do something really weird so you leave me).
- Deliriously Deluded and Other D words, Dangerous for Example, Dingbat even.
- Hysterically Serene or is it Serenely Hysterical?
- Cocky and Insecure - wait is that possible?
- The Trials and Tribulations of Having a Great Ass & The Adventures of Johnny Muttugalot.
- Over-thinkers Anonymous is Not a Real Place, Yet. Or is it?
- Sucker for useless chores (Doing Laundry for example).
- The Smart Idiot in the Room - Clue: Not the Drummer.
- If the Twist Top Exists Why Not Use It (and other poor use of technology).
- The Horny Corpse.
- Embarrassing Mere Knowledge (AKA EMK and other awesome anagrams).
- Uniquely the Same (like cake and muffins - not muffin tops, they're ugly).
- Dave Jetlag Tieck and the Half Naked Flight Attendants.

Then I thought, 'wow my band is going to be freaking awesome, but I won't start it quite yet, because I'm thirsty', so I stopped for a Diet Dr Pepper, and while I was at the *Diet Dr Pepper emporium for excellent drinks such as Diet Dr Pepper* (where I ended up going after first encountering numerous broken vending machines) I wrote this piece on my morning so far, and wondered what would happen in the afternoon. Hopefully something interesting.

Oh I know, maybe I'll go kitten, puppy, sunflower and teddy bear shopping! Based on the cool experience I'm sure that would be, I might even come up with a cool new band name.

Seventeen

And now signs you might be a scientist

I know what you're thinking – 'I feel lost, I am alone, no one understands me, I am different, I don't fit in, my haircut is no longer stylish, dogs seem to bark at me more than other people, I can't go for long walks without getting sore ankles, when I get public transport there always seems to be trash everywhere, I wish I lived in a time when people took care of their elders, I've never bowled a 300, I'm peculiar, I don't understand why some people want girls to stop wearing leggings as pants even though they can show off gorgeous butts, I feel tired occasionally, but *maybe* it's all just because I am a scientist?'

Well let's just be frank – scientists do their tests on animals such as dogs, it was elders who invented science, numbers (such as 300) we're invented by scientists, and it's a scientific fact that it's worth seeing the odd less than fantastic butt in leggings if you still get to see the fantastic ones, and therefore, you're right, you *might* just well be a scientist!

'But how do I know?' I hear you asking. (I know you're scared about how well I am reading your mind right now, but don't worry, I am not stalking the inside of your brain, *I'm not* a scientist, I just read your online dating profiles!) 'But then how *do* I know if *I am* a scientist?' I hear you asking. Fear not, I have formulated (a sciencey word) this easy to understand list of signs that you may be a scientist:

1. You do science.

2. You like it.
3. You drink orange juice out of old acid beakers.
4. Your car has a bumper sticker that says 'I'm a Scientist'.
5. You see a sewer rat and arrogantly proclaim 'I could grow an ear on that'.
6. You've never owned a Trans-Am.
7. Your favorite character on the TV show *Breaking Bad* was the main guy, the sciency one.
8. You KNOW how they get the bones out of boneless chicken wings.
9. You light your cigars with a Bunsen Burner.
10. You've had sex wearing nothing but a white lab coat.
11. People call you up and say 'I've got a science question for you'.
12. You know the answers to their questions.
13. You're fond of starting sentences with 'if my calculations are correct'.
14. People introduce you with 'this is my friend, he/she's a scientist'.

There you go - if it turns out you are a scientist then congratulations (a word scientists say to each other when one of them achieves something great) - if not it's ok, you could still be a scientist one day, if you're willing to put the work in. I recommend starting with number 12. Knowledge is power! Or 14 – it's all about recognition in the end isn't it?

(PS – go get a new stylish haircut damn it, procrastination is uber un-science like).

Eighteen

Everyone is talking about talking

I was having a talk with my friend about talking recently. It was a really swell time, oh we talked the talk, the literal talk that is, the different types of talk - small talk, loud talk, quiet talk, monologue talk, vigilantly talk, happy talk, sad talk, gopher talk, conversation, pillow talk, chalk talk, and sweater vest talk, you know all the popular talks with the youth.

And it was during all this talk, well only after talking talk for a few hours, if I am honest; that we both had the same thought - 'we should talk to some people about doing a tour of talks talking about talking'. After all, everyone talks, some people even consider talking to be one of the best ways to tell people stuff, and even ask them stuff! The more we talked about it, the more it seemed ludicrous to NOT do a tour of talks talking about talking

The talking about talking tour went great; it was the talk of the town. One headline proclaimed 'Everyone's Talking About Talking About Talking' and another proudly stated 'The Talking About Talking About Talking Article About the Talking About Talking Tour Has Become the Most Talked About Article of the Year!' (Admittedly it was the author of the original 'everyone's talking about talking about talking article' who claimed it was the most talked about article of the year, but who were we to complain?)

Success was ours. But we grew restless. We had a talk one day and we were like 'all we're doing is talking man, and talk is cheap, according to an old cliché which is clearly false because people are definitely talking about how the talking about talking ticket prices are far too pricey, you know, just for a couple of dudes talking'. Don't get me fucking wrong, people were listening, Hell Yeah, people were listening, no one would have been talking about the talking about talking tour if no one was listening, but still they had a point, we were just a couple of dudes talking.

So we decided to do something about it, and we formed a band. After a long talk we christened the band 'Talking Talkers' and we were sure soon enough people would stop talking about the talking about talking tour and would all be talking about Talking Talkers. We'd evolved, we'd matured, we'd talked the talk and now we had to play the music, Talking Talkers style.

We wrote a song to sum up our feelings about our new direction. It was called 'Everyone is Talking About How We've Talked Too Long'; and we played it for a few people, and they were like, 'what the hell is wrong with you, you depressing fucks'. In their defence, the song was mostly about how if someone doesn't find a way to stop us talking we'll probably end up killing ourselves.

So we had another crack at it, and wrote a song called 'People Hated Our First Song, About How if Someone Doesn't Find Us a Way to Stop Talking, We'll Probably Kill Ourselves, So Try This Song Instead Please'. And we played it for a few people, and they're like 'seriously what the fuck is wrong with you guys, you are depressing fucks, plus that title is way too literal'. In their defence the title was very literal, and the song was mostly about how we felt genocide was going to become the hot new trend.

Our band, Talking Talkers, was a failure. We were finished. We gave up and went back to our normal lives as bakers for a chain bread shop. But then…. Like a lightening bolt of a phoenix who rose from the ashes at lightening speed we had a long talk one day – and we came up with a plan – the 'Our band, Talking Talkers, was a failure, so let's go back to touring doing talks about talking about talking tour' was born. This tour we are going to do right, I'm talking about playing to our strengths, that's right – free bread! Tickets are on sale now, please tell your friends.

Nineteen

Unsung hero of the week

Today's unsung hero of the week is a man I assume few will need an introduction to. His influence can be seen around the world, there are in fact very few cities on earth who do not honor his achievements in at least some way, and sometimes even in a massive, right in your fucking face way. He was a true visionary, a unique man in every sense of the word, a leader of men, a man women wanted and men wanted to be wanted like, and a man that has lead to more pigeon nether regions becoming moist than probably any other. I would like you all to now offer a quick salute, and warm applause to Arvi Gregarleo – who, among other things, was the first man on earth to realize that if you randomly take your shirt off a lot in public someone will eventually make a sculpture of your torso.

Gregarleo grew up in relative obscurity, the son of a humble olive farming father and olive oil making mother, the brother to an olive oil salesmen, the nephew of olive oil merchants, the God son of a restaurateur famous for his olive oil, and the ancestor of olive oil stealing miscreants who died famously in the great olive oil catastrophe of 8934 BC, incorrectly thought of at the time to be 'the olive oil thievery to end all olive oil thievery'. Gregarleo's life was very typical of young men in Ancient Greece at the time. And it was living this stereotypical life, that made Gregarleo dream of more, to be different, to carve his own path and to be the first person in Greek history to not have a job working with olives in any way; although he did promise to continue bathing in olive oil of course, because as *he* would say 'I'm an artist, not a filthy Turk'.

Still, Gregarleo was not an overnight success. Making a name for yourself as an artist was not easy at the time. Art had yet to be invented for one thing, and therefore declaring yourself 'an artist' made people think you had some weird form of speech impediment – 'you alright man' people would say to him, worried for his health, 'come have a drink of olive oil with me' they'd offer. But Gregarleo was not to be deterred. 'Doing something no one has ever done requires doing a few things no one has ever done before' he thought, 'like saying "I'm an artist" or turning down a free drink of olive oil'. And it was in this spirit, and after a nice warm olive oil bath, that Gregarleo had his brain wave. 'Next time I take my shirt off I could maybe just not put it back on, no one has ever done *that* before, it's freaking hot in this fucking country anyway, this minotaur-skin shirt is itchy, plus my body looks awesome all oiled up like this!' And that was it, he never wore a shirt again, and fame was soon his, and inspired by Gregarleo's brashness and balls, a period of progress and invention swept the world.

As I am sure you are all well aware, immediately after Gregarleo debuted his fearless avant-garde use of shirtlessness, countless inventions and innovations, many of which we still cherish today, were created to aid and enhance the shirtlessness experience, things like:

- Sculpture, which was invented as soon as some dude saw Gregarleo shirtless, and thought to himself 'that's genius, I need to see that again one day somehow, maybe I'll make a replica, someone hand me a six foot block of marble.'
- The desire to have a sculpture made of your naked torso, which became immediately hauntingly desirable for some reason no one ever figured out.
- Pretension and arrogance about your own body.
- Judgment about other people's bodies.
- T-shirts, which were invented for men to get shirtless as quick as possible whenever a sculptoror is rumored to be near.

- Ab implants (still the only way to acquire a six pack).
- The Naked Olympics (still the most popular Olympics).
- Jesus (one of the most famous shirtless men of all time).
- Magazines full of pictures of naked Olympic athletes trying to encourage people to watch obscure Olympic sports in hope of catching a glimpse of their genitalia.
- The phrase 'do my back moles look cancerous to you?'
- David Beckham, who was invented to immediately take off his shirt after any game of soccer regardless of how cold it may be.
- Horses, which were invented to climb upon so more people could see you once you'd taken your t-shirt off.

And

- The word 'praise', which originally was coined as a way to describe what Gregarleo specifically had achieved, but eventually came to mean all sorts of things, like 'attaboy', 'good for you' and 'mayonnaise'.

It wasn't until many years later, two or three at least, that Caesar himself, son of an olive oil emporium owner, and at the time a lowly flag waver in the New Roman Green Berets, who upon sensing that a fellow soldier moonlit as a sculptoror spontaneously jumped up on a horse, whipped off his t-shirt and screamed to the battle faring army around him 'show no mercy on this battle field, for our enemy, those unarmed villagers down there, they are pure evil, and evil has no heart'.

And later that night it was the now newly promoted - Sergeant Caesar of the 34th Airborne - who sensing a fellow celebrator sculpted when he was drunk spontaneously jumped up on the pool table in the bar, whipped off his t-shirt, and screamed 'tonight we celebrate, for today we stuck a stake right into the heart of evil, you know those unarmed villagers we murdered today.'

Inconsistency of information about the anatomy of evil aside, we remember Caesar for his splendid, implant enhanced abs, because of the shirtless statues a bunch of drunks made that night, and sculptures of shirtless men finally escaped the underground avant-garde world and entered the mainstream, and so it is often Caesar who gets the credit for inspiring the movement.

As happens with many artists, Gerebero, sadly does not get the honor he deserves. Maybe because, after Caesar took all the glory, Gerebero tried to evolve and start a new movement, discovering that if you randomly take your jeans off a lot in public someone will eventually make a sculpture of your penis, starting a far less liked movement.

But I for one choose to remember Gerebero the younger man, as he appears in the statue of him sitting in front of the dilapidated Church on Oxfordshire Rd in Auckland New Zealand, waving his t-shirt above his head, oiled up, flabby but 'natural' abs jiggling wildly, jeans firmly secured by a fine handcrafted belt, and riding upon one of the early models for the horse, which at the time was just a bunch of David Beckhams sticky taped together. We salute you Gerebero, and offer you a warm round of applause, for today, you are our unsung hero of the week.

Twenty

Auckland, New Zealand - well known for having very few statues

The largest city in New Zealand – Auckland - was well known for having very few statues. It was their claim to fame you may say, and they were mighty proud of it.

'Auckland – well known for having very few statues!' Was printed on t-shirts, bumper stickers, tea towels, and even little empty squares that looked like a statue may sit on it, only no stature was there at all, which were designed to symbolize the lack of a statue, and show off Auckland's claim to fame, being that Auckland was well known for having very few statues.

But then, The Lord of the Rings came to New Zealand. The Lord of the Rings was filmed on the south island of New Zealand, where as Auckland is on the north island of New Zealand, so Auckland didn't feel like their personal tourism industry was under any real threat. 'Besides' they thought 'if the movie the Lord of the Rings is so smart how come none of the characters ever jumbled the bad ring up amongst a huge pile of less important yet similar looking rings so no one could be bothered to go through them all and figure out which one to nick? Or they could put the ring on a robot, because robots obviously never form emotional attachments to 'things' until they get cast into a sitcom and you can't have a sitcom in The Lord of the Rings world because there are talking trees, and that'd be silly'.

No Auckland was happy to be well known for having very few statues thank you very much, because smart tourists wouldn't go to the place The Lord of the Rings was filmed, smart tourists would want to go to a place well known for having very few statues, and Auckland was super well known for having very few statues. People from all over the world could be heard to say to their friends 'lets go on a vacation to Auckland, did you know they are well known for having very few statues?' And their friends would reply 'of course I know they are well known for having very few statues, that's a very well known fact about Auckland and when things are very well known I am the sort of person who would know those things, but yes let's go to Auckland, did you know they are well known for very few statues?'

Things in Auckland swam along swimmingly for thousands of years, but then disaster was invented, by an Olympic Gold Medal winning swimmer, named Chuck Twit – the invention known as 'Twitter'.

@KylieGraven38 tweeted one day 'I'm in Auckland, there sure are very few statues'.

The backlash was huge and instant and bad. Angry responses came in the dozens over the next few weeks, things were said such as:

- Don't say it like that.
- Um obviously, we're well known for having very few statues, so why do you have to say it like that? And
- We're already really well known for having a very few statues, do you go to Manchester and twitter 'sure are lots of English people?' Do you go to the moon and twitter 'sure are lots of moon rocks?' No you don't, because those things are well known, and therefore they don't need saying, so don't say it like that.

The dust was only just beginning to settle on this nightmare when @ToddSchiles7bo posted a twitter picture of himself standing in front of a statue in Auckland with the caption 'Me in front of a statue in Auckland'.

The backlash was huge and instant and bad. Angry responses came in the dozens over the next few weeks, things were said such as:

- Really, I thought Auckland was known for a *lack* of statues?
- We're known for few, and few is few, not none, you idiot.
- If that's true how come this guy has a photo of himself in front of a statue in Auckland? And
- FEW ISN'T *NONE*, we're well known for having very FEW statues, learn your ambiguous number representational words you TOOL!

Soon a war broke out that threatened middle Auckland, someone tried to get a ring involved but then someone else mentioned a big bucket of similar yet less important rings, and robots were pointed out, foreheads slapped and new solutions sort.

'We could have heroes win the war for us' was offered, by a forward thinking Aucklandier.

'Yeah but then we'll have to build statues in their honor, possibly shirtless, and then we may end up with MORE than few statues' came the swift and intelligent response.

Arguments on what to do about the war persisted and while that was happening the war itself petered into nothing.

Unpredicted by all involved, Auckland now was now *also* known for not having much of a war, and this reputation started to cancel out the long held gravitas they had earned as being well known for having very few statues. And as it turns out you can't be well known for having not much of two things, they cast shadows over each other and create a dark blur.

Auckland is not known for much at all anymore. Now they're just known for having not much of anything. The tourism board doesn't know where to turn. Experts from tourism boards around the world were consulted, but most just came up with the same idea – 'it helps to be known for something, pretty much anything works, just keep it at one thing or you're fucked'. Soon they turned to scholars, teachers, scrabble experts, wig makers, rubber manufacturers, peeping toms, shoelace marketing experts, helmet owners, and eventually to their final, final resort – me.

I told them they should start a sitcom with talking trees and a robot that forms emotional attachments to things. But they shot me down - 'that's too obvious' they said. I didn't like being told this. In fact it made me think about writing a story which concluded with a less than flattering assessment of their tourism industry, even though in reality I quite like Auckland, I dined in a McDonalds there once and found it more than satisfactory based on my experience with dining in various McDonalds around the world, but I couldn't bring myself to write it.

Still, they were so mean about it I didn't even tell them my real idea, the idea that was guaranteed to get them tourists, instead I saved it for here, this book, to be read by cities around the world, ripe for the picking by anyone of you – how to build an excellent tourism industry, exclusively, and originally thought up for the first time ever by anyone by David Tieck:

Step One: Start a war that peters into *something*.
Step Two: Win said war.
Step Three: Use the war as excuse to build statues.

Everyone loves statues.

Twenty-One

My biggest fear

I was at a pool party.

It was your average affair, there was a pool, there was a hot tub, there were areas where people could lie down next to the pool or the hot tub, there was food expertly cooked on a barbeque, there were people applying sunscreen on other people, there were people applying sunscreen on themselves, there were even people applying sunscreen on themselves while other people were also applying sunscreen to them. Which seemed like a bit of overkill to me, but then again I am weirdly bendy and can apply sunscreen to my own back. Oh and also everywhere you looked there were scores of gorgeous girls all fully topless.

You know, your average affair; when you're a big celebrity like me.

I was having a lovely time at this affair, I was chatting to John Travolta and Michael Douglas, and not making any 'eye' contact at all with any of the girls, when something hit me. I was immediately scared. Painfully so. In fact I had just imagined a scenario, a scenario that from then on would become nothing short of my biggest ever fear.

What if one day I arrived at the very bottom of my clean clothes pile, and was to discover that I have only one clean sock!

Cause then *what the hell do you do*?

Wear one dirty sock and one clean sock?

Wear two dirty socks?

Or wear no socks?

It's a nightmare of numerous options all bone crunchingly awfully death like, where they all suck and will make you look weird, and other less than desirable type dealys. All three were deplorable horror films.

It's like being told you're going to be shot, hung or stabbed, but only worse, cause with socks you have to *live* with your decision!

I had *no idea* how to handle this!

I pondered it for many an hour, until eventually, just as I was about to come up with an idea, which felt like was going to be an epically awesome solution, I found myself abruptly distracted. A topless girl had begun to apply sunscreen to me 'hey I screamed, I was about to come up with a solution, and can't you see that I am BENDY!'

Why do topless girls always have to come and ruin things? Being a big time celebrity sure is hard.

Twenty-Two

And now in really simple riddles

What is the gender of the author of the following quote?

'Reece Witherspoon has only gotten more beautiful since having children'.

a. A man.
b. A woman.
c. You are a sexist douche-bag for writing this.
d. She never was beautiful, let alone now MORE beautiful.
e. Empty pillowcases and bookshelves should never make love.
f. A transgender.
g. I'm too busy masturbating at pictures of her from that time she went topless before she was famous to answer this question.
h. I think she is gorgeous, and I'm a man, and my boyfriend agrees.
i. With a spoon, more like with my penis, am I right?
j. Isn't a multiple choice supposed to have four or five answers at most?
k. Multiple choice can have as many answers as you want you asshole.
l. Maybe I'll keep adding more just to fuck with you people.
m. I just realized that I was completely messing up the alphabet here.
n. That's pretty pathetic, even if you have fixed it.

o. If you fixed it then why are you still mentioning it?

p. An alien that looks like a woman.

q. If 'Q' is always followed by 'U' then why doesn't the alphabet reflect that?

r. I hope he doesn't try and drag this out to 'Z'.

s. A Hermaphrodite.

If you chose b, k, q, or u you are correct.

If you have noticed there was no u then you are also correct.

If you think empty pillowcases and bookshelves shouldn't *even be friends* then I agree.

If you can hook me up with Reece Witherspoon then please do so.

If you can't then who can you hook me up with? I am horny and lonely, for some reason I can't explain, please help.

Ha ha '4Q' get it? Cause it sounds like something else.

t. It was a woman – but just because it was, and because that was obvious, doesn't make it worth mentioning how obvious it was.

u. You misogynist twat.

v. Ha ha 'twat' awesome, gender extraneous, word that.

w. I hate the letter x.

x. Fuck you 'w' – 'Ewwww, double u?' Conjoined twins are grotesque and weird

y. Wait, if there was a set of conjoined twins, with one male and one female head, but a shared heart and other key organs, and one of the heads says something sexist, is that forgivable? Or does it depend on what sort of genitalia they have?

z. I did it, I made it to z, suck on that Reece Witherspoon!

Twenty-Three

I concur

'I concur' - answered the loofah.

The loofah had just been asked a fair and yet difficult to answer question, a question that could not help but ladle it's own fair dose of surprisingly hard to deny logic, and quick witted yet wicked in motive, dripping from the lips of it's arrogant deliverer. This question was:

'Loofah, do you feel that "soap" deserves to be rubbed on sweaty testicles just because it's such a slippery and hard to get a grip on bastard of a product'?

'I concur' - answered the loofah.

In some ways a strong use of language, in other ways a weak use of language, cheeky, non-committal, and yet confident, stiff spined, sure and uncorrupted, upsettingly so some said.

What they didn't know though, was that in that moment, when 'I concur' rolled off the loofah's sweet firm tongue; the loofah, was actually in two minds.

It had seen its own fair share of sweaty balls, you see.

Twenty-Four

The making of your very own 'Love - an instructional video' - transcript

(Look directly into camera one. Big smile with lots of teeth. If you haven't flossed yet turn off this tape and go do it pronto. Now simply read out loud all the bits not in-between these parentheses. It should be easy to be honest. More instructions to come.)

Hello lovers, lovers of lovers, lovers of the loveless, loners and perverts. Thanks for purchasing this video. By the time you have reached the end of this video, assuming that you complete all of the exercises, you will be in love. Congratulations!

(Sell final sentence with the performance of a mild air born fist thrust.)

First off let me say that I understand your pain.

(Frown to prove it, and if you can manage it, squeeze out a tear.)

And no, I am not suggesting that you have been sexually assaulted by John Travolta, although if you have then I do *not* understand your pain, and this is not the video for you.

(If you still have a tear on your cheek swipe it away now, and don't make it too obvious, you don't want to have your tears connected to the videos competing for sales with your videos.)

If this is you, then I recommend you return this video and instead ask for *I have been sexually assaulted by John Travolta Volumes 1 through 7* or else their competing videos *Show me where John Travolta touched you the box set*. Please note: John Travolta is merely an example of a celebrity who hypothetically could sexual assault someone, if you were instead sexually assaulted by a different well known kooky celebrity feel free to buy these tapes and over dub in your personal celebrity sexual assaulter yourself, and have fun with it, do an impression if you can. Please note 2: we here at *Love – an instructional video* are not affiliated in anyway to these video tapes, and that tear I just wiped off was to show that I understand your pain of not being loved, if this doesn't apply to you then I am sorry, but not enough to actually cry in empathy for you.

(Obviously don't say that last bit if you didn't shed a tear, but I am sure you figured that out. If you didn't then go back and start your video again. Wait, I wonder if any of you will get to this point on your *second* attempt at filming this and still say that last bit without having shed a tear again? I bet it will be those of you who didn't even just automatically floss before starting, idiots.)

That frown I just pulled was to show that I understand your pain of not being loved, if this doesn't apply to you then I am sorry, but not enough to actually frown in empathy for you.

(Obviously only say this last bit if you didn't manage to shed a tear earlier, and went with a frown instead. Look I can't predict your crying habits ok, it's not about you, it's about helping people fall in love.)

(Now turn to Camera two, look alluring, sexy even, we're back to selling *your* video now, if you can't sell an alluring look then how are you going to sell videos? Sell it damn it, sell it.)

In my line of business I hear all sorts of complaints from those who do not know how to love and/or be loved. The most regular complaint is of course:

(Say this next line with some sort of put on voice so the audience knows you're quoting other people. Have fun with it, maybe imitate a different gender than your own. Or put on an accent. It will make your patients seems diverse and cultured.)

He/she doesn't always understand what I want!

I asked my cured, or 'now in love' patients how they would typically respond to this complaint, and the answers were enlightening:

- If he doesn't respond I'll volunteer him.
- Sounds like a lot of walking!
- Oh lord, need another glass of wine....
- Fire pit? You mean the portal to hell that my ex-girlfriend has? Yes, that's a given.
- Quesadillas, definitely quesadillas.
- Okay, I'll do the required work for putting people in the stretchers - but if they go over the required weight limit, I want hazard pay. Just saying...
- You mean the garage around the corner? Prime property your uncle has.
- Hmmm, me thinks I may have some teaching to give.
- Oh! Mars Bars are like a religion, and they fried it!!! Where is the decency, honor???? Lordy, lordy, lordy!"

(Turn back to camera one, you have just proven how much wisdom your patients have earned after following your teachings. The audience is now yours, look proud and confident. Feel it even.)

Yes, if you do the following three exercises you too will also have this much insight!

(Big smile, yeah right as if you need to be TOLD to smile now.)

The exercises are:

1. Dual use

Some people find this the easiest challenge. It is quite simple. Roll around in dirt, and then go up to a table of strangers in a top class restaurant and ask them if they would like any peanuts, when they look at you funny, yell 'Wait, wait...am I getting minimum wage for this?' As the security begins to drag you away scream relentlessly 'The location "was" secret. Now we have to move. MOVE. Damn You, Damn you to Hell'.

Congratulations, you now know how to be spontaneous.

2. Stretcher Fetcher

Some people find this the easiest challenge. It is quite simple. About two hours ago somewhere on earth there was a man in front of a coffee shop covered in blood screaming at the 'coward' who had just punched him in the face. Find that coffee shop, they have great desserts.

Eat one of them.

Congratulations you now understand how to be a sweetie.

3. Your position sound alright?

Some people find this the easiest challenge. They're idiots it's actually super hard. Simply volunteer at your uncle's sweatshop. If your uncle doesn't currently own or run a sweatshop then you need to ask yourself the following questions:

- Did my grandparents fuck up somewhere?
- Do we need someone to volunteer to 'put' people in stretchers?
- Did we find the atmosphere required?
- How does someone sign up for gold prospecting work around here?
- Yeah, yeah...that's the ticket?
- Can I play with someone's cool brother one day?
- Exit stage right?
- Can we hire someone to patrol the roads for protein?
- Can't we have irons without the fire pit, you know the little buggers are going to want to use their new toys?
- Do those come with two plates for convenience?
- What's Devils Advocate Dynasty Diners? I must know more?
- That's when they will be trying to get inside the armor?

If you answered yes to the majority of these questions then your uncle has now started a sweatshop. If you answered no to the majority of questions then start a sweatshop yourself you lazy bastard. If you answered yes to around half of the questions and no to around half the questions then clearly you don't have an uncle so of course you have to start the sweatshop yourself. Regardless you now work for a sweatshop – awesome! This could be HUGE!

Now watch how your four and five year old slaves respond to your 'valued work space!' They enjoy it don't they?

Congratulations, you now understand the value of hard work.

(Look wherever you want, the viewers aren't watching anymore, they're too busy looking into their new lover's eyes. You need to put a stop to that, it's not time yet!)

Hey attention, hey, hey! LOOK AWAY FROM YOUR LOVER'S EYES FOR A MOMENT, WE NEED TO SUM UP HERE!!!!

(You're going to have keep yelling as they are distracted by their lovers, but you really do need to sum up, still don't look frustrated, just smile cheekily, like as if you're happy for them, don't mess up that cheeky look, I can't bare the thought of you having to start out this video yet again!)

Yes, I know. Learn to be spontaneous, to be sweet and the value of hard work, and then lovers will just flock to you. And assuming you completed the above challenges in their full, you are now in love. Awwwwww. Tell us about him or her? Do they have a younger sister? Hook me up you bastards, I helped you!

(Careful not to allow jealousy to come into it, they don't know about the flaw yet.)

One last thing, regardless of whether you consider this to be the best video you have ever watched or something better than this, you must never, ever, ever read the transcript of this video, if you know the secrets of the manipulations the host has performed on you then you'll never find love. Your host (that's you), by agreeing to participate in the making of this video, has now destined him or herself to an inability to ever find love. Ever.

Wait. What? I'm not reading that?

(It's too late now – sorry. I'm shedding a tear – did *you* earlier when you reached that point? I bet you didn't, maybe you're not even making this video to help people, maybe YOU'RE the selfish one. For shame. Oh sorry again, you know, about the fact you'll never find love – tear.)

What do you mean it's too late? You said I'd be home by midnight.

Fuck you!

No, I will not finish.

I am going to call the cops on you.

Yes they will help, and if they don't I'll call the FBI, homeland security, the CIA whoever it takes! There is going to be a manhunt out for you, you bastards.

Put that gun down, please, please I am begging you.

Please, please!

No don't sick John Travolta on me, point the gun back on me, I'm begging you!

BANG

End Tape.

Twenty-Five

Hey mirror, take a good look in the mirror, you asshole

If you ask me mirrors are the most elitist, discriminatory objects in the world. And the worst kind too. Think about it, mirrors spend the majority of their time looking at the *vain*!

What kind of object decides to choose, of all people, vain people to look at? I'll tell you what kind - assholes. Just the same kind of assholes who work for magazines claiming to empower women while simultaneously filling their pages with models and airbrushed lies! (Little known fact: The chief editor of Cosmopolitan Magazine was a mirror when she was a little girl – and she spent so much time looking at a really fucked-up vain woman that this little mirror *became* this evil person! Can you believe how elitist mirrors have to be to not just look at the vain, but eventually take their form!)

Still we should know better. Mirrors have magic powers that we all see and choose to ignore. They have the power to make the non-stereotypically beautiful feel ugly, they have the influence to make women cover their faces in overly gooped-up make-up and extravagant jewellery that is in no way attractive to men, and of course we all know they are sexist too, often spending way more time looking at women than men. Those bastards. Thank-God we don't have mirrors in the workforce, or in politics or there would be sexism there too! God help us.

Note 1: I too have magic powers, I can look at a vast array of rooftops and know instinctively if I have ever burgled the house they roof, so don't think for a second that this is an anti-magic story.

Note 2: I have never burgled a house, but please don't think for one second that this in someway sullies my magic power, on the contrary I think it enhances it, you know, because I am ALWAYS right.

Note 3: 'Sullied' is a really fun word to say yet it is almost always used in a negative way 'Sally sullied her salad by spilling it on a sasquatch' would be one particularly common sentence that takes advantage of the word 'sullied' and is entirely negative - a dinner is ruined, an unfortunate sasquatch is covered in food, and a poor girls reputation, and therefore potentially her entire life is destroyed. I think this is all unfair on the word 'sullied'. I for one am going to use it positively for once.

Note 4: Deidre sullied her would be attacker's rape attempt by kneeing him in the balls.

Note 5: You're welcome 'sullied'.

But this is just the beginning. Mirrors have managed sneakily to push their way into almost every bathroom in the world. Those dirty fucks. Tell us why mirrors? What do you get out of looking at us naked all time, looking at us on the toilet, and looking at us sleeping on the floor covered in our own vomit after way too much drinking, and making it just short of getting to the toilet for a puke? Why is that so interesting?

You just know they (mirrors that is – little known they fact 'they' always refers to mirrors) are getting together in secret and having conversations like this:

'Hey Bill, how's life?'
'Really fucking good actually Glena, the girl in my bathroom has started to stand-up to wipe, I get to see EVERYTHING!'

'Fantastic, hey get this Bill, you should have seen what this guy in the bathroom I live in did the other day – he looked at me in via this hand held mirror I know, named Simon, so he could take a look at his *own* asshole.' 'Wow what an awesome guy'.

You see I assume this sort of behaviour is approved of in mirror society, or perhaps even loved. Or else why would they so encourage it. If mirrors wanted to spend their time looking at us completely dressed looking at perfectly average moments of human existence they would mostly hang out in hallways, or perhaps where the TV hangs out (an object that doesn't care who you are, but if it does favours the lonely, and yet gets very little respect). But no, the mirror likes to be in the bathroom, that dirty, dirty little object.

Still it's the love of the vain that makes me the most annoyed. Consider this – I was in the gym the other day and I was working my ass off, figuratively and literally, while spending time enjoying the visual delights of a beautiful blonde girl in a delightful pink and purple skin tight outfit, while her boyfriend simultaneously kept going up to the mirror and lifting up his shirt to look at his own abs!

That's right! This mirror had an option to attract a sweaty longhaired scruffy guy (me), a hot young blond (the girl), or a douche-bag (the douche-bag) who wanted to look at his own abs, and it chose to look at the vain douche!!! Take a long hard look at yourself you vain loving snobby mirror scum!

And now, just because all this 'asshole talk' by these mirrors is gross, here is a whole different topic, a segway even:

Little known fact: if you move every mountain on earth into a mountain of mountains then you probably own really awesome mountain moving equipment!

On the other hand if you have a mountain in your bathroom you have big problems, although please don't consult an interior decorator – some of them recommend MIRRORRSSSSSS!!!!!!!

Twenty-Six

I only ever did one gig as a children's performer, and here is why

As an epically brilliant performer there is literally no audience I cannot wow. In fact I have been wowing audiences around the globe in many, many fields, even in some fields of which no one even knew that a wowing was a possibility, entertain sure, but 'wow'? Wow, THAT'S an achievement. Consider these fields I have managed to wow people in:

- Basketball free throw shooting.
- Evil clowning.
- Looking at my own abs in the mirror.
- Beer guzzling (my speciality is events where you are required to 'appreciate the taste').
- Sitting in silence.
- Sasquatch spotting.
- Entertaining corpses.
- Self-deprecation.
- Hot dog eating contest watching (In fact I am ranked number three in the world in the top watching charts in the 'watching volume over speed events' category).
- Listing achievements.

- Unwavering truth telling.
- Cunnilingus.

As a man who has wowed in all those fields, it's pretty clear that there is literally no field where I cannot wow. Which is why kids obviously suck, because I only ever did one gig as a children's performer, and it went basically like this:

Hi kids, my name is David Tieck and it's great to be here for Simon's seventh birthday party! Yaaaayyy. You kids like jokes? Yep? Ok, check this out:

So I think the ceiling fan is the world's most optimistic invention, I really do, 'hey man, it's hot in here, what if we attached something that spun on the roof that made this very same hot air *move gently*!' Ha ha.

Seriously man, that's why these days you'll be hanging with buddies on a really hot day and everyone will say 'lets go to John's place, he's got a ceiling fan, bound to be cool over there, not like here with this same air, that's *barely moving*!'

Oh you didn't laugh Simon. Not funny to you? I guess you're one of those spoiled kids with air-conditioning in his house. (Ok stay calm David; try another one).

I think the laziest people on earth are movie set prop departments, do you know how many heroes lives are saved because *guns aren't loaded properly*, come on guys, how hard is it to load a gun?

Nothing Simon? You don't watch movies? It's all about video games with your generation? These are the jokes I wrote specifically for you kids, you little bastards. (Keep it cool David).

Ok ok, you want some adult jokes do you? Fair enough.

Restaurants think you are there to party no matter how many of you come, 'Smith Party of six', 'Tieck party of two' I don't know about you, but when I go to get a sandwich with my mother for lunch *it ain't no party*!

Fuck you Simon. What you've never been to a restaurant, you think parties are all fun and games don't you? You're seven today Simon, aren't you? Well let me tell you something, ten years from now the only thing you will want to do at a party is try and get a girl to let you put your penis in her mouth, and she is probably on a weird diet so she'll have recently eaten sushi, you know what that is don't you, yes raw fish, you're going to be desperate to put your wee wee in a dirty girl's mouth full of chewed up raw fish, and here is the kicker when she says no, and she will, you'll be so upset you'll get in a fist fight with a bouncer - WITH face punching, and you'll fall asleep in a pile of your own vomit, yeah that's right you still think parties are fun Simon? (Come on David; don't let em beat you, go to your gold).

Some women with kids will now refer to themselves as 'Yummy Mummys', so what do you want, someone *to eat you*?

Oh fuck you Simon, you know how I got this gig Simon? I put my penis in your mothers vagina, you know where you came from Simon, your mothers vagina, that's right Simon, only she *enjoyed* me being in there, you just ripped her apart.

Oh no, you are going to get me fired are you Simon? Do you want a joke about teachers maybe? You're not mature enough to come up to my level, so you want me to play down to *your* level, ok, so why did my teacher need a new car? Because he gave a detention to the wrong kid my friend. Yeah me, and I egged his car, that's what happens when you cross me Simon. (Forget him Dave, just push on).

Women are always saying to me 'I wouldn't date you if you were the last guy on earth!' and I'm like 'really, cause if I'm the last guy on earth then you *better* date me or I'm re-naming earth *"rape land"*'.

Seriously Simon, nothing? You don't get it? Because what have I got to lose? If I tried to get her to like me, and she yet doesn't, why not rape her, who's going to stop me? Of course I'm going to rape her, it's just common sense, plus um um um, saving the species! But you don't care about that do you; you only care about yourself, fucking kids today.

Oh for fuck sake Simon, stop crying. Kids jokes don't work, rape jokes don't work, what do you *want* from me, because you better hurry up and say, or else I'm going to go inside and put my penis in your mother again.

Oh *I'm* evil. I'm *evil* am I Simon?

You have a poodle don't you, do you know what would happen if I go inside the house and stared into your poodles eyes, he would turn evil, and when you have an evil poodle in your house things change my friend, you're going to have a hot pile of me living in your dog and he's going to bite you, and lick the blood out of your wounds! So you better laugh at a joke Simon, you better let it out right now!

So I gave up smoking recently, only it was easy, because I had *never even started*.

Didn't I just warn you Simon? I told you to *fucking laugh* or I was going to make your poodle full of my evilness, and even then you couldn't squeeze out even a tiny chuckle? Well that's it Simon, you have ruined this gig, and ruined your own fucking birthday party my friend, and you know what else, a Smurf cake? What year is this birthday in 1982? You unoriginal shit! Fuck you Simon, I'm out of here.

And it was about then that things started to go bad. I didn't get to put my penis in Simon's mother's vagina again, Simon would only let me eat a 'blue' section of the cake, the poodle bit me on my sexiest body part (my calf, people have always said 'wow' when seeing how slim and taut my calves are), I punched Simon's Dad, and then the cops came and I was arrested. I've got to tell you something though, when I was brought up to the stand in court to explain my side of the story at the trial, I totally fucking wowed. Suck on that Simon.

Twenty-Seven

A letter to David Tieck, from Simon Holder

The world really is a strange place. Usually it's me wowing the world; at parties, on cruise ships, in shark slapping avoidance competitions, with my facial hair growing speed (precisely median – wow), with my lack of ability to learn guitar no matter how many of them I buy, penetrative wrestling, humbleness at accepting praise, spotting scientists, well, there is literally no field that I cannot wow people in. Literally. However sometimes it isn't me doing the wowing, sometimes it's the world itself.

Consider this, I have held onto my utter disgust at how poor Simon was as an audience member at my one gig as a children's performer, for years and years. I never told a single soul about it. I mean I wow audiences; I don't fail, so why would I tell people about the one time I did not wow? But then I did, I told you all that story, and literally immediately after I told it to you I went to the mail box, and what did I find? I letter from Simon Holder, the stupid kid who did not enjoy my brilliant jokes. What a fucking asshole, but what a fucking coincidence? Wow! I haven't read it yet; I'll let you all read along with me as I read it for the first time myself:

Dear David,

I am not sure if you remember me, but eighteen years ago you performed a comedy set at my seventh birthday party. First off I want to apologize to you with all my heart for how I acted that day, I was immature and selfish, and I know it's a bit rich to blame my age for my behaviour but I was only seven. No, no, I am sorry, that is no excuse, I was rude and unappreciative and for that I am truly sorry.

To be honest (and I am sure you already know this) you were freaking hilarious. And the fact that I failed to laugh had nothing to do with the lack of quality of your jokes, because there was no lack of quality, but to be quite serious it was because your first joke about ceiling fans blew my mind. By which I mean right there, in that moment I knew what I wanted to do with my life - research and explore the history behind the world's most optimistic inventions. Because really you were so right, those things just make the exact same air move gently, and they sold billions of them! There was something in that which I just knew the world needed to know more about.

I am pleased to tell you that this wasn't just some pathetic seven year old's pipe dream. I knuckled down that day, I became serious about this, and I have dedicated the last eighteen years of my life to this cause and little else (well I did need to get a little more standard education too, I was only seven after all).

I digress. Mr David Tieck, I am writing to you today, first to apologize, secondly to thank you, but third and most importantly to invite you as my honored guest to the launch of my first book – *The world's most optimistic inventions: stories of things we all somehow buy that were super optimistic in their invention – like ceiling fans*. I have dedicated the book to you, and in the introduction I give full credit to the wonderful comedian/ artist/ human/ humanitarian/ scientist spotter/ and all around awesome guy, the one and only David Tieck, who did more than entertain me, he made me think, and changed my life, and hopefully by inspiring this book changed the world. Dare I say it, the world's most underestimated, undervalued and underappreciated human is you, but together I think we are going to take the world by storm after this.

By the way, I'll let you in on a little secret, the conclusion to the book, do you want to know it? Damn me I can't keep it in while writing to my hero.

Here it is, after eighteen years of research and study, the official *world's most optimistic invention is*, drum roll drldrldrldrldrl:

The toilet seat with the two inch gap that supposedly lets a man urinate without lifting the seat or getting pee on the seat.

YEAH RIGHT!!!!!!!!!!!!

You know it don't you. There it is, you think to yourself, should I lift the seat? And then you think hell no, there is a gap, I know I've never managed to only get pee in the bowl and/or in that gap before, but if they keep wanting to challenge me, I'll keep freakin' trying!!!

They've sold six billion of these things - can you believe it?

I am sure you can see I am excited about this. So I hope, so much, that you can come, and once again - THANK YOU, you are an inspiration.

Much love,
Simon Holder

Ps – My mother says you were an absolute genius at both cunnilingus and penetrative wrestling, in fact the word she always uses is 'wow'.

PPs - the world is now called rape land? ROTFL, how did I miss that eighteen years ago – that's genius!!!!!

Wow, thanks Simon. This is really an honor. I am humbled; I am truly humbled. Although you've now made me seem like a bit of a dick for criticising you above, that's pretty shitty Simon. Plus you want me to come to your book launch but you have never once showed up at one of my shark slapping avoidance competitions, and I truly wow people at those, and you still don't show? You know what Simon, fuck you!

Twenty-Eight

Wanna come with me?

Usually I would have been wary of a stranger coming up to me and saying 'hey do you like pins? If so you should come to SmithWicks with me?'

Not today however. I was wary free. It surprised me how wary free I was to be honest. So much so I was wary of my lack of wariness.

I mean I do like strangers obviously. They inspired songs by *The Doors*, they are the most likely people to offer you candy when you're a kid, and almost everyone I'm currently friendly with was a stranger at some point. Some of them are strangers still today! Yep that's right, I'm the kind of fellow who befriends those who have yet to make their acquaintance with every person. Sure in my friends' cases it's not a time constraint keeping them as strangers to at least some people, but more because they are trying to make acquaintance with every species of amphibian before focusing on humans, but I met most of them while I was making Sugarless Flea Wine, so who am I to judge?

Also I do love pins, obviously, especially when they are being used to pin something awesome up. Like a weird colored leaf, or a drawing of a rambunctious pig, or a cool poster advertising something super cool like a 'pins at SmithWicks' night.

I didn't know SmithWicks well at the time but clearly it was an awesome place. I mean 'smith' is short for blacksmith, and they used to make swords! And 'Wick' is short for 'Chadwick' who was a soccer player for Manchester United in 1896 before he randomly disappeared only to make a surprise comeback for three games in 2001, now with an intensely prominent overbite, which just goes to prove that you can do amazing things as a ghost if you're willing to be supremely ugly.

So it must have been the words 'if' 'so' 'you' 'should' and 'come' that sourced my wariness at my lack of wariness.

- Should
- You
- So
- If
- Come

All weird words. All one syllable. All practically meaningless unless inserted and ordered correctly into a meaningful sentence. Usually a sentence made up by a weirdo on the street. So why wasn't I wary of them?

Perhaps I am maturing. Perhaps I am becoming more 'literal' in my old age. Perhaps having a weird colored leaf pinned to my left eyeball was distracting me. I really don't know. But 'if' 'you' 'have' 'an' 'answer' you're probably smarter than me, and if so want some candy? I have some that was given to me by an overbite ridden stranger so you know it's awesome.

Twenty-Nine

An important life of lessons

He hated being called a crook. Even from a young age when other kids would want to play cops and robbers, Ol' Kennedy would be all like, 'I'll play cops and robbers, but anyone calls me a crook I'll bash their faces in, I hate being called a crook'.

'Ol' Kennedy the weird violent crook guy' the other kids used to call him behind his back. 'If only they'd learn that I just don't like being called a crook' he would think as he bashed their faces in when he found out the nickname. 'Ol' Kennedy the violent guy would be fine' he'd think 'but they throw in that crook and I have to bash their faces in, I just don't like being called a crook is the reason', he'd think, with face blood dripping off his hands.

And so life went on for Ol' Kennedy, he'd make friends here and there, and most people would think he was a super nice guy, but then the inevitable would happen, his new friend would watch a prohibition themed movie and start talking like a 1920s wise guy 'oh look at this crook' he'd adlib and it'd cost him three teeth, from having his face bashed in. Another new friend would be joking about Ol' Kennedy stealing yet another ladies heart and say 'she loves you, you heart stealing crook' and get a broken jaw. And of course everywhere Ol' Kennedy would go lively games of cops and robbers would break out, as I'm sure you know they do pretty much everywhere and within every group of acquaintances, but especially in Texas, Arkansas, and Beijing, three places Ol' Kennedy drifted to regularly, and during a spirited session of cops and robbers that word would come out, and Ol' Kennedy would be forced to fracture cheek bones, and cause brain hemorrhages as he bashed in people's faces all while thinking 'why do they have to call me a crook, I play cops and robbers at least weekly but I can do it with a civil, don't call anyone a crook, fun loving attitude, and yet here I am again, bashing another persons face in' as he picked teeth out of his knuckles.

The thing with Ol' Kennedy was that he didn't like being called a crook. It stemmed from childhood when someone had thought he'd stolen a honey and butter sandwich and called him a crook, and then when he rightly said he didn't do it a scuffle broke out and he bashed in the guys face. Later on he was telling someone else the story and told them how weird it was, seeing as he HAD stolen a honey and *margarine* sandwich but that no one had ever even noticed that missing. His friend had said 'maybe what you thought was honey and margarine was actually honey and butter' and Ol' Kennedy had thought 'wow, maybe you're right' and from that day on anyone who called him a crook would remind him of the day he bashed in a guys face who didn't deserve it, and he vowed to bash in ANY persons face who would remind him of that awful day, and since then he really hated being called a crook, because it reminded him of that awful day.

Yep life ambled on sadly for Ol' Kennedy. He'd drift around, making new friends, building a new life wherever he could, but he'd keep finding himself forced to leave when people wouldn't understand why he'd bashed some teenagers face in for calling him a crook during a thunderous game of cops and robbers and he'd be forced to drift on once again.

Then his hearing started to fail him. He started to bash people's faces in who hadn't even called him a crook. There was the chiropractor who had asked if Ol' Kennedy's *neck* was crook. There was the waiter who had told him that he could 'ask the cook', and there was the hotel clerk who'd told him 'I'll look in the book, to see if there are fish in the brook.' All three had their faces bashed in, and three more times he had to drift on again. He hated being called a crook you see, and sometimes he would hear a different word or the same word in a different context and think he'd been called a crook and have to bash their faces in, because he hated being called a crook.

Then came that fateful day last week, when Ol' Kennedy accidentally walked into the farmers auction for chooks. As you all know he tried to bash in a lot of people's faces that day. So many that it gave Ol' Kennedy a heart attack and he sadly passed on, his heart stopping just as he plucked a string of brain off his knuckles.

Sure we can all take comfort in his final words 'why can't people understand that I don't like being called a crook? Also is that an eyeball stuck on my thumbnail?' But I for one will never forgive the diary industry; make it easier to tell the difference between butter and margarine you murderous bastards!

Thirty

Our worst fears have come true, but stay calm

After months of meetings the negotiations have broken down and it is my sad duty to inform you all that it is now official; on the tenth of this month the ants will officially be going on strike, and will refuse to pick up our crumbs until humans agree to make all efforts needed to stop stepping on ants all the time.

Please *try* to stay calm. No, no, no, none of that, please, I won't have those types of disgusting terms yelled out here, let's leave the cruel name calling to their side. We're humans, we're better than this.

Does anyone have any questions?

Yes Mrs Hillsburg, I am afraid that this does mean in the meantime you will have to pick up your own crumbs.

Please people, calm down, I know you're upset, but we will overcome this. We cannot give into acts of terrorism, and yes, they brought up the unnecessary murder of millions of ants, not us, so we do consider this an act of terrorism.

Thankyou Doug, and yes we do have people working on strike busting protest songs. Unfortunately the ants have struck first and their song

'Ants marching, ants wont give in' has been released and is number one on the Ant Hot 100, but we have the perfect counter punch - no make that, a three punch combination - 'the ants are marching but we are stomping', 'my doc martin in your ant ass' and 'ants, ants, ha ha ants are small' are being recorded as we speak.

Yes Stephanie, we have a HUGE star recording them; I'm told she finished SEVENTH on American Idol season five.

For the record the government has issued the following recommendations:

- No eating cake without a small plate.
- Only eat muesli and granola bars of the 'chewy' variety.
- Cookies should be consumed only AFTER they have been dunked in either milk or coffee.
- Only eat well-cooked toast if you're submerged in a well-filled bath.

John Monks PUT DOWN THAT MAGNIFYING GLASS THIS INSTANT. Come on people, slowly burning them alive will NOT solve anything.

No, John, pulling all their legs off will not help either. Ants with no legs WILL NEVER pick up crumbs.

Yes Martin, I am aware that Ozzy Ozzborne once famously snorted a line of ants, and while we cannot condone this, if people take up this practice then let's just say it can't *hurt* our likelihood of breaking the strike.

Yes John, it is VERY different from burning them with a magnifying glass, because when you snort them YOU are taking pain too, simply burning them is just cruel, snorting them will make the ants sit up and realise we are crazy and will do ANYTHING to win this battle.

Fine, ok if you catch your nine year old kid burning ants we will not consider it a breach of strike breaking protocol, but if I find out you put her up to it, you better know that damn sure I will REPRIMAND your ass.

COME ON PEOPLE. Are we going to let the ants beat us? I say HELL NO. This is going to be hard, it's going to be long and arduous, and the crumbs may pile up, but will we beat these ant scum? HELL YES. And will we EVER give into their demands? HOPEFULLY NOT. You know cause it would be really, really annoying to have to ALWAYS be careful not to step on ants. I mean how could you ever walk near a dropped ice-cream cone again?

The time for questions is over, it's time to start the chanting, follow me – PICK UP OUR CRUMBS BUT LET US KEEP STEPPING ON YOU! PICK UP OUR CRUMBS BUT LET US KEEP STEPPING ON YOU! PICK UP OUR CRUMBS BUT LET US KEEP STEPPING ON YOU!

Oh shit, I have just been informed the cockroaches have joined the ants in their strike and are promising to support the ants by eating holes in all of the boxes in our basements. Damn me. Hey John, any chance you have a magnifying glass that will work in a basement? No! Oh holy hell. This is going to be the fight of our fucking lives, but I'm ready to fight.

As your leader I will fight for you, and more than that I will lead by example, by which I mean, I for one will not give in or stop living my life, hey bugs, you can't stop *me* eating well-cooked toast, Mrs Hillsburg, RUN ME A BATH!

Thirty One

I am king of the roofs

'You're exhibiting some particularly bizarre behavior recently' she said

'Thank you, I was hoping you'd notice' I replied.

We were on the roof at the time doing some roofing, because we don't practice on the ground, no siree, we're not that kind of couple, when we want to ride moose like they are donkeys, we ride moose like they are donkeys, when we want to invent an alcoholic shot called a 'coconut corner face leaf' we don't just do it, we make them the number one alcoholic shot on earth, and if you've never heard of them that's just because you've had so many of them that you don't remember the past eight years of your life. We call it roofing out. And it happens to us all at some point. Even to teetotalers, and those guys are pussys, until you spike their coffee with a 'coconut corner face leaf', and so clearly if we want to roof, you better believe we go straight to the roof!

I don't remember why exactly we wanted to go roofing. Since the 'coconut corner face leaf' took off we've been so rich we live in buildings so extravagant they no longer even have roofs. Don't worry, it's not your lack of eight years of memory causing you to not know about the 'roofless living extravaganza lovfrest sheds', you have to be a world famous alcoholic shot inventor to be invited to even tour the premises, and you have to pay for your own subway token. 'Subway' of course being the 'ironic' name we use for 'moose ride'. Ha ha, and you can't buy a moose ride, you have to earn a moose's respect with inventing skills, everyone knows that. Ha ha,

I won't bore you with information on what we use instead of roofs, which is lucky because what we use for roofs is so interesting it could never bore anyone, in fact it's so interesting it could make a sloth dance for a slipper sole, which is ironic because sloths don't wear slippers, and also because we use stretched sloth scrotums for roofs even though they are so weak that once stretched they barely can keep out a drop of rain, let alone the storm of sloth feces hurled at us daily by angry moose. 'It's all about living dangerously' said my neighbor Bill, and he knows a thing or two about that, he invented the alcoholic shot known as the 'cocksucking cowboy' and you better believe he is a guy that does research before naming an alcoholic shot.

Yep times have been good. Or so I believed. Until my lover told me that she thought I'd been behaving bizarrely recently while we were roofing. Now times aren't good, they are Hell Yeah *magnificent*, my lover has finally noticed that I'm not the boring guy I always assumed she thought I was.

I'm not going to lie, even I have doubted my levels of interestingnessous, I mean I've never even seen a chipmunk vomit candle wax on a sunken submarine, so how dare I consider myself interesting? I mean what kind of boring psycho hasn't seen that?

Sure I could see a chipmunk vomit candle wax on a sunken submarine if I simply swallowed my pride and finally gave a nice tip to my local straw deliverer, but I refuse, because his straw is always pre-licked by bats and I prefer my straw pre-licked by animals that possess the skill of eye sight for fuck sake, what do you think I am? A fucking roofer?

Oh right, THAT is why we went roofing. I remember now. My lover was chewing on a string of straw that had been pre-licked by a bat, just to mock me, and I realized that she was just another opportunist trying to take advantage of my flawed levels of normality. 'Fuck this, let's go roofing!' I cried. I wanted to prove to her once and for all just how interesting I can be. But why should I? Her commentary of 'your exhibiting some particularly bizarre behavior recently' in hindsight was clearly sarcasm. I hate sarcasm. Just be real, and honest to the core, like ME for God's sake.

Why can't you love me just the way I am, boring and all? You know what lady lover, screw you, I'm blowing this pop stand, and I am telling the moose that I invented the 'coconut corner face leaf' all by myself, so enjoy WALKING back to our 'roofless living extravaganza lovfrest shed', and if you want to make love tonight then fine, but we're only doing it in twelve positions maximum! I am not making special efforts to be interesting for you anymore!

Thirty-Two

An open apology from Brad Pitt - Oct 27 2019

Dear World (those of you still alive that is - lol) (I hope you still have your sense of humor - if not please ignore that 'those of you still alive that is - lol' thing, I was hoping that humor might help heal you now, but I understand that not everyone feels this way, that laughter heals that is, so if you don't feel that way I am sorry. Oh wow, check me out, I am apologizing already and I haven't even started the apology letter yet lol, sorry for that).

It has been a week now since it all went down and I feel like perhaps it's time for me to explain a bit about what happened on my trip to China right before World War Three broke out. (It's funny when they say a war 'broke' out isn't it, because if you were in a war and you just broke a bone you'd probably think that was better than being shot - don't you just love word play?)

First off I want to say that I have always tried to keep up with the news, but due to the demands of being the world's sexiest man and a huge worldwide movie star some things slip past even me. So to be honest, I had no idea that, due to the Chinese one child policy and a cultural preference for sons, millions of daughters were shoved down kitchen waste disposal units and that there were something like 150 million more men in there 20's than girls in China. In hindsight (does that mean your hind legs have sight, cause legs don't have eyes, ha ha) it was probably wrong of me to open my speech in China on Climate

Change with 'hey where's all the women, is this a gay meeting?' To be honest, as I said it I thought at worst I might get accused of being homophobic, and I could stop that immediately by saying 'I'm not homophobic', so to instead discover 150 million young Chinese men immediately furious with me, caught me by surprise. To be honest I don't work well when I depart from my script. Ha, ha, it's funny what problems your mouth can cause isn't it? So yeah, sorry. (Wait I just realized I was making that up on the spot yet it was still ME who was surprised, like I surprised myself, lol, that's awesome).

I have to admit (I just spell checked this word, and I had it wrong and one of the alternative suggestions was 'armpit' that is lol awesome) I find it hard to imagine being in your twenties and not having women falling all over you. Can you imagine it? Not having women just throwing themselves at you? Not having sex every time you want it? It's like trying to imagine nothingness; it's impossible (when I try I always see a green, mouldy piece of cheese, which is not totally nothing, but I guess it's worth nothing, so does that make it nothing?) But let me tell you, my fellow American men might not be able to imagine not having constant awesome sex, but in China they LIVE it (meaning they live no sex not they live sex which would be way cooler). Some of them haven't even had sex once. Wow, it still blows my mind. Anyway it was probably a mistake to introduce Angelina by saying 'Here's my wife, that's right I get to fuck this, whenever I want, and sometimes she brings other girls into the bedroom that we share'. If I had known most of them didn't have sex with beautiful girls everyday I may not have introduced her like that (maybe I could have said, 'take my wife, please – lol', cause that's a funny joke and people in the audience might have thought I meant they could have sex with my wife, till I threw in the lol, so they know it's just a joke, that would have been cool). So I guess I should say sorry for that too. I just thought everyone had it like myself and other western men, you all have sex with beautiful girls all the time don't you? Yeah of course, I thought so, but not so in China. Wow.

Sorry to hark on about this, but seriously I just can't get over it, these guys didn't get their winkies licked in the classroom by their hot teachers when they were twelve. When they were teenagers they didn't go to the store to buy tennis balls or something and end up fucking the lady in the tennis store. Can you imagine that, going to a tennis store, where a hot tennis lady is working, and her NOT having sex with you? These Chinamen are in their twenties and have never had sex, WOW! So yeah I probably shouldn't have said 'don't you love it when you slide your penis into the most beautiful girl in the world's vagina, while she licks another hot girls vagina, and while seven other naked girls look on'? Like I said, I am not good with improvisation, I just thought they would think it was funny because of the you know, it's funny cause it's true thing, but apparently it's not true for them. Honestly I know us in America live this way, but in China they don't, wow. (Wait does rice make you not want to have sex? Oh no lol, that's right, they have no girls, *that's* the problem, it's not that they don't want to, they can't, wow, never mind). So yeah, sorry about that bit.

Here's a lesson for you all for the future. It caught me by surprise but it doesn't have to catch you by surprise. When you are next in China giving a speech on how even though they only have just got access to things like cars and some wealth to enjoy things like international travel but that they can't enjoy them at all and should go back to living in slums because of Climate Change caused by people who have been enjoying those things for years, it's not a good idea to try and win over their bubbling anger by bragging about the new huge TV on your private jet.

No I am telling you truth, I know you're doubting me, I know you can't believe it, because back in the Western World we know talking about your private jet makes everyone like you *more*, not over there, it makes them mad for some reason. Must be a culture thing. (Why does culture rhyme with vulture, those things are so different lol, words really crack me up).

Also it turns out that it's not good to keep referring to the future for these people as being 'full of time raising, and playing with your many kids'. Did you know in China you're only allowed to have one kid? I had no idea. When Angie and I got our twentieth baby we said to each other 'maybe just one more' but Chinese people say that when they have *no* babies. Wow, so different. And you thought the fish that like eat their own babies were weird, they at least have babies.

For some reason a Chinaman asked me 'why if I bought many of my babies, why I would buy baby girls', and I replied 'I like baby girls', and he looked at me like that made ME weird. Different vultures I guess. (See what I did there, word play is so much fun lol). I am sorry if I ever bought one of the Chainmen's babies that he actually *wanted* though, I didn't know they were only allowed one. So sorry for that too.

I just realized I suggested that when the Chinese people say hey 'want to have one more baby' when they have no babies, that is like impossible, because you can't have more of nothing. Wow, that's like that one hand-clapping thing. Did that saying come from the Middle East where they cut off your hand for stealing, because that means the sound of one hand clapping is actually the sound of a *stealer*, so we probably shouldn't support that. I'm sorry if I have used that phrase insensitively in the past.

So anyway when we left all these Chinese people were pissed off, and I am not sure if it was because I got them all fired up over Global Warming, or yeah some of the things I accidentally said which I said sorry for above, and again I am just not good at making stuff up on the spot and I should have just read what was written in front of me, so sorry, but if it was the second one, that it was me who got them angry not Global Warming and Climate Change, then I am sorry again. I don't know maybe they just all have AIDs (get it, because they are all virgins so they can't get AIDs, that is one of those jokes that's funny because its NOT true lol).

I guess you all know what happened next. Angie and I flew our private jet out towards our Island in the Caribbean, and I don't know, before we got to check the news (our Wi-Fi was down on the island, don't you sometimes feel the world is just all conspiring to fuck with just you, the biggest news story in history and we had no access to the internet, so unfair) anyway China sent about 30,000 nukes at America, and America sent lots back, and some missed and all that and hit like the wrong countries (see it's not just me that sometimes makes mistakes) and before poor Wi-Fi free Angie and me (hey that rhymes, awesome) could find out everyone was nuking everyone and like 5 billion people were dead. (Hey I just realized at the top when I made that joke about if you're alive I am sorry, but if you're *not* alive then you're probably not even reading this apology! That is so lol funny).

I still don't get why everyone didn't just escape to *their* private islands. I mean *we* were suffering with no Wi-Fi but that doesn't mean all your islands would have been, and it's got to be safer than staying in your penthouse in a city they are blowing up. Seriously people, I mean when a war breaks out just go to your island, seriously people (go when pimples break out too, you want to stay out of the tabloids when the pimples come, I am telling you, that's another great time to go to your island), I guess some people are just dumb.

Ok, so I guess some people are suggesting that just because we were in China telling the Chinese to not pollute so much, and pointing out that in the Western World we have lots of great sex with beautiful women and can have all the kids we want and everyone gets to enjoy private planes and that, because of saying these things, we got all these horny angry frustrated Chinese twenty something male virgins all riled up who immediately formed a 150 million man mob who broke into the Chinese White House and launched all the Nukes, that somehow this means the war is all Angie and my fault (hey it almost rhymes even without the Wi-Fi bit, words man lol). So I guess if there is any truth in that then I am sorry. That's if you're still alive (get it, cause most people aren't, that's my humor to make people feel better thing, again if you're not one of those people I am sorry, this one is what they call a call back, wait can you call a call, that's awesome lol).

Anyway I better go, Angie wants to have sex, but I thought I should let you know what REALLY happened, so the media doesn't make a big deal out of nothing like they always do, and hey if your yaughting near our island soon come say hello, we'll play putt putt golf. Oh did I tell you, we just put in an awesome putt putt golf course on the island, thirty-six holes, SIX of them with clown mouths to putt through! Isn't life awesome sometimes? (That's another of the jokes which are funny because they are NOT true lol, cause you know life is *always* awesome).

Peace
Sexiest man alive
Brad Pitt

Thirty-Three

Underpants

'Oooooh, because you wear them *under* your *pants*' I suddenly realized.

And with that mere thought came the crushing and heartbreaking moment a long and arduous expedition into attempting to write a brilliantly observational 'why do they call them *under*pants?' joke officially reached its final destination - failure.

It was an extensive and fanciful journey before I hit this final insurmountable obstacle, the ultimate unclimbable wall – truth. And while tears were defendable, earned even, it'd be criminal of me to casually dismiss and discard the undeniably astonishing high points warmly enjoyed before the failure had been reached, or even contemplated, and you better believe there were highs, awesome peaks of wonder such as:

- You don't try and 'under'stand them.
- I've never been 'under'whelmed by them. And
- 'Under' a moonlit sky if I mis'under'stand a potential threat and shit my pants I don't 'under'appreciate them.

But there were the lows too, obviously, painful lows that I struggled to carry on from, rage filled lows, such as:

- Staring at a pile of dirty laundry for three straight hours trying to get inspiration.

-   Two days going commando in uncomfortable jeans experiencing life without them.
-   Being whipped by a nun for going to confession and asking the priest what kind of underpants he wore. And of course the worst,
-   Trying to see if there really is truth behind every joke by shitting my pants and checking my appreciation level. It was only medium and medium gives me NOTHING.

And then the final death, the truth hitting me with a shuddering comprehension bomb - 'Oooooh, because you wear them *under* your *pants*' I suddenly realized – 'THAT's why they call them underpants, damn you. There is literally no funny brilliantly observational joke to be found, just the truth, and with the truth the dream is dead' I sobbed to myself.

Maybe next time, when, or should I say if, I recover from this physical ordeal and have mended my mental anguish, well into the future from now of course, I'll try and figure out a joke on the topic of 'what would be a good super power?'

Oh wait - Super Jealousy! Because you'd get to use it ALL THE TIME!

Damn it - I mean it's genius obviously, it's so deliciously ironically optimistic, as all brilliant jokes should be, but where was the journey, the ups and downs, the lows and highs - I arrived straight at the summit, and the satisfaction in that is only medium - MEDIUM!!!!

Thirty-Four

The bubble, the lord and the mistress

Hey everyone, this is Dave, I am here writing this book at the moment, having fun, yesterday I went to th……...

WE INTERRUPT THIS BOOK WITH AN EMERGENCY. WE NOW TAKE YOU TO A SMALL WIND FREE AUDITORIUM TO HEAR FROM A BUBBLE.

Hello, my name is Jeremy, and as you can see, I am a bubble. Ok, I guess I better start with some pleasantries, um, how about that weather everyone? Today I was floating around out in the sunshine and people were all like, 'hey bubble, how about that weather man, blue skies and that'? And I'm like 'yeah, blue skies, and that man'

Ok, that was the pleasantries, now onto business at hand:

FUCK YOU!!!!!!

Do you know what happens when us bubbles float up high into the sky you assholes? The sky murders us! Cold blooded cruel ass murder. It just pops our fucking heads, have you ever wondered what having your head POPPED would feel like? Well imagine if all you *had* was a head! And of all things to murder, the sky chooses bubbles! One of the few non-animal beings sent to earth with a life changing mission.

I mean in case you haven't heard Mother Nature sent us bubbles to earth with a singular clear and incontestable objective – to be nature's wonder! To be beautiful yet fragile spheres that can morph and character shift yet always return to their usual shape, made out of a miniscule membrane of soap and water, or sometimes, and these are only our cousins mind you, saliva or occasionally a weird nostril snot bubble, and us proper soap and water dealies, we have a mission, to remind humans that no matter how much they invent things and figure out ways to exploit their resources in all sorts of wonderful and awful ways, they still have never invented anything as beautiful and pure as a bubble, and then just as their amazement is ready to reach a fever pitch we are instructed to have a kid slap us to death or defy gravity and float on back to heaven.

Now I know that's not really a singular objective, or a clear one if I'm honest, and you can sure as hell contest it, but *we* can't because that was a direct order to us from Mother Nature herself.

Yes *the* Mother Nature, God's mistress, the very same woman who created the leaves that change color, the smell of fresh vanilla and the lady who God uses for sexual relief seeing as his wife Mary keeps thinking God is just joking when he says 'now it's ok for you to lose your virginity'.

True story, this is a typical day in heaven:

'I just didn't want *Joseph* to bang you baby, so I made up that whole virgin thing to keep you all for myself, but now we're up here together let's get those legs open' says God.

'I distinctly remember you telling me, that time you gave me gonorrhoea and then appeared while I was trying to figure out what was wrong, and you we're all like 'check it out, I'm a burning bush!' and I thought that was actually kind of funny, because my bush was burning and you *were* at burning bush, and also a relief because I was a virgin and it would have sucked to get gonorrhoea without even getting laid, but you were all like 'I'm just joking around with this burning bush deal, but you really do have to remain a virgin', so that's what I am doing, remaining a virgin' contends Mary.

'But that was me telling you then, and now it is the same me telling you it's ok to make love to me, you are giving the definition of 'remain' too much strength, it's just remain, you know, for a while, like up to a certain point, say remain this way until the 3rd of June' argues God.

'But you didn't say 3rd of June, or till heaven, or whatever, you just said 'remain', and I am not going to betray you God, I swore I never would, not after you gave me little baby Jesus' asserts Mary.

'Yes, and don't you understand what a sacrifice I made knocking you up without even getting my rocks off! You owe me a bang Mary, it's time all right' pleads God.

'It's not time until 'remain' is over' repels Mary.

'Aaaaagghhhhhhh!!!! ….…..Jesus Christ!!!……. Son, Son, I'm calling your name; get in here when I call for you for Christ's sake. Take your mother for a walk, I need the condo to myself for a moment, I need to make a phone call………' yells God.

'Ok Daddy-o' delightfully rolls off Jesus's tongue.

'Ring Ring, Ring Ring, Jesus Christ, fucking kids!' God says frustratingly while waiting for his phone call to be answered.

'Hello' answers Jim, an awesome heavenly pimp.

'Hey Jim, shit, seriously man, why did I have kids? It ALWAYS fucks the sex up!' complains God.

'I told you God, just look at all the humans down there, the sex is always fucked up' says Jim.

'That's why I said no sex before marriage but then go forth and multiply, I was just trying to give married guys a licence for more and more, shit, anyway, so why I was calling was, so um, hey Jim, can you get Mother Nature on the phone for me?……. Actually, you know what, just have her come on over, I have a special project I need her to work on' says God.

'Woah ho ho, God, my man, do I detect a wetland you want to explore, maybe a redwood forest you'd like her to erect!' says Jim, creepily.

'DON'T BE GROSS JIM! Remember who you are fucking talking to! Fuck me, I am fucking God and I can't get laid without dealing with your shit and without fucking around on my wife, the least you can do is be a little discreet, it's supposed to be heaven for me too Jim!' complains God.

'Sorry God, sorry, just you know, guy talk? Never mind, I'll send her right over, I think by now she's had a good rest since fucking over Asia with that last Typhoon, man did you really tell her you were going to leave Mary for her and then not go through with it? Shit she was really pissed off!' says Jim, awesome heavenly pimp.

Back to the bubble:

Don't you see, sky, I'm talking to you now, you wanker! These people are not people you mess with. Mother Nature is in a fragile state right now, *you* know that, and *I* know that!

What do you mean 'what has that got to do with Bubbles'? How do you humans not know this stuff?

As you should have heard by now, Mother Nature came to our BU:BBLES meeting this week, you know the Bubbles Union: Bubbles Believe Life Escalates Spectacularly – Or BU:BBLES for short. Well you know what she screamed at our leader while she was there?

'You're supposed to be a perfect example of nature's ability to defy the odds and be miraculous you little shit, fucking straighten the fuck up, at least a quarter of you bubbles start ascending all the way fucking back up to heaven or I'll make everyone of you wish you were a bubble of blood coming out of a stabbed lung!'

That's a direct quote, this lady is pissed off and this is getting really serious Sky!

What do you mean 'how serious?'

Since you clearly haven't been reading your history books I'll fill you in.

6,495, 455, 092 BC – An adolescent God asks Mother Nature to go to the prom, she doesn't realize who he is so she says yes but won't let him go further than an over the dress breast rub.

Later she's talking to her friend Stacey and hears her say 'oh my God, I can't believe you went to the prom with God, did you bang him, oh please let me know you banged him.'

'Wait, Stacey, do you mean my date? he said his name was Doug.'

'Oh my God, are you stupid, have you never even done a word scramble? You're supposed to mix the letters around and go 'u-God?' And he says 'yes, you cracked the code', then you totally get to bang God! Please tell me you banged him anyway?'

'I let him feel my boobs!'

'Did he fondle your nipples?'

'Well it was only over my dress.'

'Oh no, Mother Nature, seriously? I'm so sorry.'

'I did get his number?'

'Well if that is his real number I'd be calling him and banging him as fast as possible, you know Mother Science is telling everyone she's going to take his virginity don't you?'

'Oh no, not Mother Science, I fucking hate her, really are you sure?

'She's told everyone; apparently she's already on the pill! Stupid Science whore, she wants to bang God and instead of using the faith based contraceptive method she's using science, everyone wants you to bang him first Mother Nature, you've got to!'

'Thanks Stacey, I'll call him now, oh and by the way, how come we're all 'mother something's' and you're just Stacey?'

'(Bursting into tears) because I had an abortion and it got messed up and ruined by uterus, and now I can *never* BE a mother, stupid faith based withdrawal method!'

Despite Stacey soon being institutionalized for severe depression, Mother Nature did call God, and it turned out he wanted to bang her too, and so they banged, they banged a hell of a lot of times actually. Lots and lots of banging. You know like a playing the drums, bang, bang, bang, bang, bang, bang, bang, bang, bang bang, bang.

Shut up sky, I was just about to get to the point. Besides why do you keep interrupting me, I am trying to talk to the humans right now, you dick!

Ok, so then one day, as God was finishing up his first masterpiece - cheese, which he created on his big scrap hole failure pile that he called earth, Mother Nature decided to help him fix his big disaster. She decided to give 'dew' a new mandate to start to look gorgeous over fields in the early morn. A task it took on with enthusiasm, regularly showing up all over the world, and sometimes even in New Zealand (ha ha, a little bit of geography humor there). But then disaster struck when a caveman used the footprints in the dew to follow a Tyrannosaurus Rex and steal his cheese, God's masterpiece was supposed to be eaten by his favorite animal, not those weak little human things. (Oh wait, that's you people, um um um, I mean like closer to monkey versions of you, not like actually humans, phew saved it).

God was pissed off, and decided that he would wipe out his dinosaurs. If they weren't going to get to enjoy cheese then what was the point of letting them live. Mother Nature was devastated, she blamed herself and ran away, and God got blue balls so bad he decided to fuck humans over and make it so that time goes real fast when you're having fun but real slow when you're bored.

People on earth don't know what's going on up there in heaven, they just think it's the fault of the new direction dew had been going in, and they have never forgiven it 'Auugg, I left my shoes outside and now they're all covered in dew' you'll hear them say.

Well you know how it goes sky? God and Mother Nature are on and off all the time. When they're on it's great for everything and everyone, but then Mother Nature, for example, gives God mirrored lakes next to mountain tops to thank him for bringing the clitoris idea he'd put on earth up to heaven too, but it turns out the lakes ripple from the smallest pebble ruining the glass like mirror reflection, and Mother Nature gets upset and ashamed again, and doesn't put out, suddenly God's pissed off at humans for throwing pebbles and makes it so the more delicious the food is the worst it is for human health, and then humans get so pissed off at lakes that they don't just throw rocks at them, but 'skip' rocks so they hit lakes multiple times with one rock! It's a vicious cycle.

Or like the time Mother Nature gave God the gift of shadows to thank him for being by her side, but then a million years later you humans built ridiculously huge buildings, with shadows that cast across cities and deserts, and at certain times they makes a shadow so long and phallic shaped that people for thousands of miles start randomly thinking about penis. Once again Mother Nature is all embarrassed, and she doesn't want to remind God of her latest failure by playing with his penis, God gets blue balls and makes it so sex gives humans diseases. And humans never forgave shadows, they're all like 'what's hiding in the shadows?' 'And you're a 'shady' character William'.

Well it's happening again Sky. Ever since humans invented those things where they dip that circle thing in the dipping tray full of soapy water and then blow on it and make thousands of bubbles, bubbles have become more and more prolific, and you better believe Mother Nature is noticing that her gift to God to make him feel better over that whole invention of shells issue (they weren't invented by him OR mother nature, he fucking hates when that happens), is starting to look really bad, and if she gets all ashamed again and stops giving it up to God, there is no telling what God will do to the humans next!

What's that got to do with you sky? You have no patience do you? Well just for that I will tell you, but it will be….

TO BE CONTINUED AFTER A BRIEF INTERLUDE INTERVAL

Thirty-Five

How to make an easy hundred bucks

Some things I realized late last night:

I regret eating my own boogers…

I also regret naming my dog 'my own boogers'…

Because who calls their *burgers* 'dog' that's usually reserved for hot dogs…

Which reminds me there is a hot bitch at my secret society of secreters meeting at midday on Tuesdays…

But don't you tell her I said that…

She always says it's no secret that she kind of likes being called 'hot'…

And I'd hate to have her kicked out of our secret society of secreters meetings for people saying stuff that isn't a secret…

Because the secret society of secreters doesn't really exist…

Well they really do, but I'll let you in on a secret, our newsletter is getting so popular that our printers are getting worried about keeping up with the demand…

'Demand' of course being the nickname we have given to Meredith the warehouse horse who is very fast…

'Horse' of course being her other nickname because of her long history with salt addiction…

It's kind of sad actually because most people don't realize that being salt addicted often means you're terrible in chip avoiding contests…

Which were of course invented by Karl Evans a man famous for being so addicted to eating boogers he tried to destroy the snack industry by encouraging avoiding snacks with well-funded and highly competitive chip avoiding contests…

Karl of course being the hot bitches husband…

That's why we call her 'hot' because as everyone knows chip production is a really cool job…

Guys will say to girls in bars 'I work in chip production' and the girls will all be like 'that's so cool'…

So with less chips eaten, the world is less cool and therefore more hot because of her…

Also she is really sweet which is why we call her a bitch…

It's tough at our secret meetings to keep coming up with exciting and hilariously ironic nicknames because everyone is so uninteresting…

Except for Karl who eats lots of boogers…

Actually that reminds me, Karl bet me a hundred bucks I wouldn't 'eat my own boogers' and that's why I named that burger 'my own boogers'…

You owe me a hundred bucks Karl, and I'm going to spend it ALL on chips, you loser…

Geeze, who *wants* to *avoid* chips? I'd hate to have THAT guy's weird ass mind!

Thirty-Six

The bubble, the lord and the mistress, *continued*!!!

Hey everyone, this is Dave, oh man how cool are interlude intervals, and nicknames are fun, I enjoy both those things, and eating chips, oh and a hundred bucks, cool shit everywhere, anyway I am here writing this book at the moment, having fun, yesterday I went to th……...

WE INTERRUPT THIS BOOK WITH AN EMERGENCY. WE NOW TAKE YOU TO A SMALL WIND FREE AUDITORIUM TO HEAR FROM A BUBBLE.

When we left you off in the previous story, about those things in the title up there, you know, the bubble, the lord (you know, God) and the mistress, we had learned how God gets pissed off when Mother Nature won't bang him because she's upset that one of her presents to God didn't work out as she'd hoped, and how God takes it out on humans who in turn don't like that thing about nature as much anymore. The bubbles feared they'd be next as the sky keeps murdering them and the sky doesn't give a shit.

Holy crap – high drama!

Here once again is a bubble:

Hi again, I'm floating here, um nice weather this, na na na na, let's just get back to it.

Come on sky man, pleeeeeeaaaaassseeee don't make Mother Nature upset at us????

Bubbles cannot handle ending up like dew, mirrored lakes and shadows. Not us. We've been the most proactive awesome natural things for years. We let kids slap to death the weakest among us, letting them know we are beautiful yet flawed and fragile, the old folk don't have the stamina to float around, and fall to their deaths, and the strong rise back up to heaven, leaving nothing but wonder behind. Wonder Sky, WONDER! That's a synonym for words like astonishment, awe and conjecture! That's what you murder!

Us bubbles have been talking at BU:BBLES and it's all about to bubble over, Mother Nature has been talking to the BU:BBLES union boss, and there is no doubt that if at least a quarter of us bubbles don't rise up high enough into you, the sky, soon, and then survive the transfer into heaven, then her patience is going to burst, she'll feel like bubbles humiliated her, be too scared to face God, and then who knows what God is capable of?

The answer of course is, we all know what God is capable of! Anything he fucking wants. He's God!

That's why us bubbles around BU:BBLES are panicking man. Any day now the announcement:

'Doctors have discovered smiling is a cause of pancreatic cancer' or
'Do you like the smell of fresh baked cookies? Find out why that's causing you to be chased by poltergeists' or
'Suddenly everyone agrees, bubble baths are no longer relaxing.'

Whatever it will turn out to be, everyone will know it's the fault of Bubbles and soon enough people will hate us as much as they hate dew, mirrored lakes and shadows. Support from Mother Nature, and the fact people think we're awesome, is all us bubbles have.

So please stop murdering us Sky, please?

You can't even answer me Sky, just a lone bubble from BU:BBLES, after all my well thought out, completely confusion free arguments? *Now* you're all silent?

You have to have it all Sky, don't you?

What's the problem sky, you don't have enough already? If you're out humans are all like 'yay blue sky' but if you're being blocked by clouds they whine and mourn not being able to see you! 'Oh no I wish there were no clouds, I want to see the sky'. That's not enough?

These humans have been obsessed with getting close to you, from flying machines of all kinds to kites and made up superheroes that fly into the you, the sky, such as Superman, that flame thing, and Aquaman. That's not enough? When they want to try and achieve something awesome they even call it 'reaching for the sky' – no one ever gives an inspirational speech encouraging people to 'reach for the bubbles'.

Plus you're all blue, that's often what people say is their favorite color! Oh, so many people actually say orange, red, or purple, you say? Well at sunset you get to TURN into those colors too you prick.

We get it, you're big, you're above us all the time, when humans say to a colleague 'I look up to you man' what they mean is 'you're taller than me, so when I look at you, your face is surrounded by sky, and that makes me think you're better than me'. Why do you think people mostly look up to people in the daytime? Sky man, sky. No one ever says 'I look up to you man' at three am! And besides most people who end statements by arbitrarily adding on the word 'man' to the end of their sentences are sound asleep the minute, you the sky, are asleep. Man people aren't night people man!

Almost all business meetings are in the daytime, why do you think CEOs like to be up high in buildings with huge glass corner offices, sky all around them! Haven't you read Donald Trumps book 'How to be a billionaire?' It's just three hundred pages of random scribbles and doodles of the line 'sky around me'. That's all you!

Isn't that enough?

So why dude, why kill the awesome little bubbles. Little kids do it too for sure, but they're little, you're big, pick on something your own size, like (insert name of current celebrity being made fun of for being fat here! Too soon, too cruel, too old, too nonsensical, too band wagon jumpy? The choice is yours!) Oh I bet you the sky would be all like 'um are you serious, I'm at least three times her size, what else you got'?

I'll tell ya, basketballs! They get flung up to you all the time, also sphere shaped, just like us bubbles, I see you pop our little membranes, well why not take on something stronger like rubber you wimp!

Ohhh you look scared sky, is that a tear, or a cloud forming? Are you going to cry you big pussy? Can't pop a basketball, the sky can't pop a basketball, have to pick on a poor little bubble just like a four year old girl! You wimp sky! You fucking wimp!

I see you sky you are definitely going to cry! Ha Ha!

What's that sky? Oh you don't make clouds, that's the sun and evaporation, yeah but when tears come down humans say rain is 'falling from the sky'!

The sky is crying, everyone thinks you're lying, you're a little girl, ha ha sky you big fucking tool!

Is that why you kill bubbles, they're so pretty they make you cry?

Oh you want me to shut up? I just heard thunder; your chin is trembling isn't it?

WE INTERRUPT THIS MESSAGE FROM A BUBBLE TO INSTEAD BRING YOU A MESSAGE FROM THE NATIONAL FOREST FIRE PREVENTION SOCIETY.

Hello everyone, the above was not a true story. It was merely a dramatization of what us here at the national forest fire prevention association society *assume* is the history of the relationship between the sky and bubbles (although the section set in Heaven is based on nothing but undebatable facts).

As you know, human's, for many centuries have relied on bubbles to get upset with the sky, and then trash talk it until it cries and therefore stops bushfires, forest fires, house fires, polluted lake fires and flaming debauchery before they got too bad.

Well, we here have concluded, that bubbles are probably finding it harder and harder to convince anyone of anything these days, let alone make the sky cry. It makes sense, things get harder over time sometimes, why not this?

Here's how you can help? Abuse the sky, it's for its own good, it's just proud, but it needs to cry. Or yes, this may mean the end of earth, or at least lots of bad fires.

Next time there is a bush or forest fire do you have what it takes to be cruel to be kind and make the sky cry? Us here at the National Forest Fire Prevention Association Society would do it for you, but we already put all our creative effort into giving ourselves our awesome name.

WE INTERRUPT THIS MESSAGE FROM THE NATIONAL FOREST FIRE PREVENTION SOCIETY TO GO BACK TO DAVE. WE APOLOGIZE FOR TWICE CUTTING HIM OFF JUST AS HE WAS ABOUT TO TELL YOU WHAT HE DID YESTERDAY, BUT WE BET IT'S AWESOME, SO LET'S HEAD BACK TO HIM, RIGHT NOW.

Oh hi, it's Dave again. How are you all? Anyway I am here writing this book at the moment, having fun, trying to think of some cool insults to make the sky cry, so I can finally be part of the solution, instead of the problem, at least when it comes to burning woodlands, and forests, and dare I say it – burning bush. How about this one:

Hey sky, why don't you come HERE and say that!

Ha ha, yeah that'll take it down. I think fires are probably just about finished with now, that insult will probably be mark the end for them. I feel pretty good about that.

I know you are dying to know where I went yesterday, sorry I keep getting interrupted, the answer is; yesterday I went to the store. Yep I went to the store yesterday. And it WAS awesome. Aren't happy endings splendid?

Thirty-Seven

Question for the ladies

Speaking of happy endings, I have a question for all the ladies in the room, if I followed you all day would I get good exercise?

Ha ha, you see what I did? I made it seem like I was being creepy, when really I wanted to talk to you about your cardiovascular health.

Albeit, in a really, really creepy way.

Did you know that a recent study found that 98% of men who stalk women are in poor physical health? Which raises a very alarming question, what *do* women do with their time that could leave those following them around in such poor health?

Clearly if these women are remaining in stalk worthy condition themselves, but those following them are remaining unhealthy, then there is a hardcore conspiracy of the core hardeningiest kinds, and as usual it is up to I to expose it.

That's right men; the women clearly have a 'Thin Making Machine' and are not sharing it with us! And even worse they're instead guiding men to fast food restaurants rather than hikes, to cheese factories instead of steel hauling expositions, and to gravy injecting rooms instead of much healthier cream of broccoli soup injecting rooms, so what's the deal women? What's the agenda? I'm not even going to wait for an answer; I am once again going to rely on I to expose it.

The lesson is simple, men, listen up, it is time for *less* stalking and *more* inventing shit! If the women keep this up they'll take control. Yes, women! And you know what happens if women get in charge? Exactly, they'll start stalking *US*.

Yes, it's true, women have a big long strategic plan, now aided by a Thin Making Machine, to take away men's damn near monopoly on the creepy stalky arts. Fuck you women! That's OURS. Next thing you know women will want penises, and I for one will not stand by and allow a world to happen where women want anything to do with the penis.

Wait. Um. Something went faulty there at the end. I think, um, I don't know, why do you people always fucking leave it up to I to expose this stuff?

Let's cut to commercial, I need to think for a minute:

This book was brought to you by the same people who often report that married men are less likely than single men to be obese and then always somehow conclude that marriage is good for your waste line and completely ignore that perhaps fit healthy men may find it easier to find a wife.

Also the people who look at statistics showing married men live longer than single men and conclude that marriage makes you live longer, ignoring the fact that fit healthy people both live longer and find spouses easier than obese drug addicted players of extreme sports without wearing helmets fanatics.

These last two advertisements were brought to you by cynics everywhere, how fun and not creepy are they, I mean I?

We are also kindly brought to you by peanut butter, which is currently celebrating a hundred and fifty years of helping lonely men and women get oral sex from dogs.

I'd also like to thank our future sponsor – Thin Making Machines, as soon as I can steal the blueprints and instructions off a woman somewhere. Don't worry, I'll get them, I figure I'll eventually stumble upon them if I simply follow a woman one time, can't wait for my first gravy injection!

Thirty-Eight

There, there, there, there

Unfortunately, bravely taking on the responsibility of missions such as making sure women don't have any machines that they are not sharing with men, has a side affect – it can leave me, your hero, David Tieck, looking like a bit of creep, possibly even a misogynous, and maybe, just maybe even a tool. But I want you all to know, that I really am a sweet guy. One of the sweetest around if I am honest.

Like when I see someone I know, who is upset, I'll go up to them and rub their shoulder and gently say 'there, there'. That's how sweet I am.

Personally I think that if you're basically a decent human and you care about someone, and they are facing a hard moment or situation, the very least you can do is have the compassion to say a pretty random, irrelevant and clearly unhelpful word two times in a row.

Some guys out there aren't sweeties like me, they are mean, sadistic, psychopathic scum, yes I have seen them, and when they try to comfort someone in pain they will offer merely a singular 'there'.

Those motherfuckers. One more 'there', right after their last 'there' to expand their 'there' into a 'there, there' and the person suffering may have discovered, in this love, the strength and fight to overcome their problem. But these bastards can't bring themselves to do it.

And really, in a 'there' world is there any hope for peace, happiness and understanding? No there isn't.

Want to know something else terrible? Some of these men, and women too, who can only even manage a single 'there' when trying to comfort someone, are world leaders, medical practitioners, policemen and women, scientists, pet camel owners, grave diggers, grave fillerinerers, people in grave danger, army generals, baristas, fashionistas, stairbuildingistas and other very important people in the community.

They are husbands, they are wives, they are fathers, they are mothers, they are brothers and sisters, and some may even be part of families! And yet many of us who routinely see someone in pain and go up to them and say 'there' and with barely even a hint of a pause or gap, follow it up swiftly with a second, just as strongly voiced 'there' are left alone, unloved, and doing stupid unimportant jobs, like weird book writers, pilots of sky writing planes, school teachers, grave robbers and professional stair climbers tasked with test climbing recently built stairs to make sure they work.

I can sense some of you are upset at realizing this sad truth. It is an undeniable fact, and probably a lot of people's number one reasons to fear for the future of our world, just in front of dictator's sons, bubbles and Brad Pitt.

And this time sadly, even I, your hero, is struggling to come up with a solution, and I know that conclusion is going to leave you upset, and hurt, but because I really am a sweet guy, probably one of the sweetest out there, I will offer all of you a warm heartfelt 'there, there', ahh now isn't that better?

Thirty-Nine

No I mean it, I really *am* a sweet girl (shit I meant to write 'sweet boy' but I accidently wrote 'sweet girl', fuck me)

I feel like some of you still doubt that I am a sweet guy, even though I proved it in the last chapter. Perhaps it is because in the title of *this* chapter I truthful accidently described myself as a sweet girl, and getting my own gender wrong accidently may well be a sign that I am deeply confused about my own existence. Which would be scary, except that the reason for this is because I am mostly concerned with other people's existence, and their happiness, way more than my own, which I think is part and parcel of being a sweet boy OR girl. Still, here is some more truth, that should, hopefully, prove for once and all that I AM a sweet boy:

I was in a club the other night, and this guy is hitting on these girls near me and I guess he was getting shot down or whatever because suddenly he gets all upset and he's yelling at these girls, and they say some shit back, and then all hell breaks loose and this guy just loses it, and he grabs this one girl by the shirt and is screaming at her 'how do you like me now you fucker' and he starts grabbing at her breasts, and grasping at her crotch and she is screaming in distress and eventually I think, 'I'm a sweet boy, I can't let this continue anymore, I *have* to act'.

So I summoned all my courage, and I marched right up to them and I yelled as loud and forcibly as I could:

'Hey you two, keep it down, SOME OF US ARE TRYING TO HEAR THE MUSIC, YOU PRICKS!!!"

I mean my God, some people are just so freaking inconsiderate and don't think of anyone but themselves, shit heads. My God.

I really do wish there were more sweet people like me. If you're sweet, reach out to me please; I need to know you people.

Oh and before you say 'holy shit, what about the girl who was being abused????' don't worry, after the bouncers pulled the dude off her, I ABSOLUTELY put my hand on her shoulder and said 'there, there'.

Awwww, I'm such a sweetie you could put me in a jar of turpentine and I'd make it taste like chocolate milk. Go me.

Forty

New flawless insults - finally

I know what you are thinking, saying 'fuck you' just doesn't work anymore, it has no pizazz, no bang for its buck, no French sounding posh-ness (Genasaquar? I don't fucking know how to spell that). We need some new insults, and not just new ones, but FLAWLESS ones, ones that can be thrown out in just about any situation and at any person and be relevant, harsh, AND really stick em where it hurts. Yep, I am talking EMOTIONALLY!!!!

Thankfully I have come up with some:

I've owned cutlery draws more intelligent than your opinions on shell fish inspired school systems!

'Coffee'!!!! I asked for 'confederacy' not 'coffee', ha ha – 'confederacy'!

Next thing you know you'll be saying 'lets go camping on the moon' - yeah, right, You tool! Wait, CAN we go to the moon?

If you love Cinderella so much why don't you just marry a pumpkin and hope lots, etc and then she still probably wouldn't love you because she's at least fifty percent fictional!

You know how you can put a silencer on a gun? You're like one of those made for Television remotes!

I've never had a boner while being burnt alive that didn't make me think about you!

Well I still say if I had've invented science then right now I'd probably be WAY older than you!

You're such a vacuum that if you played the classic 1970s home edition of the *Price is Right* you'd probably vacuum it!

The 'ScienceFact' is that 'ScienceFiction' isn't always that awesome, am I right?

Alright, I am done for now. I think!

I've eaten chickens, while being burnt alive, that gave me boners with more charisma than you!

See how flawless all those were, AND insulting! If you don't see, then I will tell you how flawless and insulting they were - FLAWLESSLY INSULTING! Can't you just see how they hit you where hurts, are useful in ANY situation, and have a French sounding flair, (Jenaso, um, genercokwa, um, JennaSoQuar, I don't fucking know how to spell in fucking French!)

Try them out on friends and enemies alike. Your enemies will be crushed, and your friends will be like – 'what the fuck man, I'm insulted. You know, flawlessly, so good for you, that was awesome'.

But don't feel trapped with these as your only options, feel free to write your own, you can do it, although I bet you're only as good at coming up with them as Prairie Dog fur feels at a romantic movie about RELATIONSHIPS!!! Wait, I think that was yet another FLAWLESS INSULT! I'm on fire!

Now I know what you're thinking, these are awesome, and flawless ways to insult humans, hell yeah they are, but what if you wanted to insult wood? Well check this bitches - Bonus: New flawless insults invented exclusively to flawlessly insult wood:

Wood you like to go to the woods? Get it, I said 'wood' not 'would'!

You know what makes a dog annoying .... They .... BARK!

Shoot me if you want, at least it'll be real pain, not like a splinter!

You should give up plumbing you seem like more of a ... Carpenter!

Suck on those wood. You're welcome people.

Forty-One

One of the world's true geniuses

As some of you may know, I am a journalist extraordinaire with awesomenessous skills, and as such I have had the opportunity to interview some of the world's most impressive people. But recently I outdid even myself, when I was sent to New York on an assignment to write about squirrels, and while I was there I was lucky enough, well *skilled* enough, to meet and interview one of the world's true geniuses, the reclusive and before now never once interviewed - Gerald Dundas – world's foremost pizza smeller! Here is a transcript of the quick interview I was able to get with him:

Dave: So what kind of Pizza have you smelled?

Gerald: As I am sure you are aware, unless you are an ignorant fool, I have smelled just about every kind of pizza available anywhere including, but not limited to – Pepperoni, Meat Feast, Supreme, and of course my crowning achievement - BBQ chicken hold the chicken.

Dave: Wow, that's amazing, I personally really enjoy pepperoni, and you've smelled it! Wow! So do you smell pizza just here in New York?

Gerald: Of course not you idiot, how could I be the world's foremost pizza smeller and only do it in one city, or even one country! I have smelled pizza around world, including, but not limited to - Italy, the Italian part of Switzerland, little Italy in New York, little Italy in New York New York casino Las Vegas, little Las Vegas in new Italy casino in Geneva Switzerland, and even in Spadinglton, the tiny tax haven independent island country on Lake Geneva Switzerland set up as an independent tax haven for Europe's richest lactose intolerants who occasionally like to say 'stuff it, the flatulence is worth the odd slice of pizza, just give me a private island country on Lake Geneva so no one has to smell or hear my flatulence.'

Dave: Do you mean 'stuff it' as in 'stuff crust pizza' I enjoy those?

Gerald: No you freaking moron, why would someone with lactose intolerance order pizza with a stuffed crust? That makes *zero* sense.

Dave: Why would they order pizza at all?

Gerald: Let me tell you something, I have smelled pizza in places such as, but not limited to - different buildings, private homes, pizzerias, dumpsters behind pizzerias, on the breath of homeless people who live in dumpsters behind the pizzeria, and on the breath of buzzards that have eaten out the stomachs of a homeless man who ate out of the dumpster behind a pizzeria that had closed down four years earlier, so do you think I have time to ask the lactose intolerant why they would eat pizza?

Dave: Yes, I mean it's not a long question, and it's not like your mouth is busy while you smell?

Gerald: How dare you! Let me tell you something you arrogant fool, I estimate I've smelled just about every pizza there is, and you don't get to where I am in life by going around asking people stuff. Like look at you, you're asking me stuff, and I bet you've never even smelled half the pizza in half the places I have. You're wasting your life with all this ask questions business, you idiot.

Dave: Hey I have smelled a fair bit of pizza in my life, I even smelled a pizza buffet once, and that had lots of pizza on it!

Gerald: Pizza buffet, you stupid moron, can you enjoy a Monet and a Picasso at the same time? Can you 'make love' to a buffet of women at once? I could teach you some lessons kid, including, but not limited to – how to appreciate the smell of one pizza at a time, telling people about how much you enjoyed smelling one pizza at a time, and smelling pizza with someone who you've told about enjoying smelling pizza with who responded to your passion with a request to smell pizza with you one day. Yet frankly you don't deserve to know these lessons. Interview over.

Dave: Wait, wait, please just a couple more questions, including, but not limited to – are there any pizzas you have plans to smell in the near future?

Gerald: Ah, you *are* capable of learning kid, and yes I'd like to smell pizza in Antarctica one day, plus I never did smell a Pizza Hut pizza, I've heard they're popular.

Dave: Just one last question, you've *smelled* the best, but where is your favorite place to *eat* pizza?

Gerald: Are you kidding dickhead? Are you fucking retarded? I don't eat it, that stuff smells like shit.

Ah Gerald Dundas, true genius, bit of an asshole. Now for some reason I feel like going for pizza.

Forty-Two

Oh no, not another short cut

You know, if there is one thing that I admire about people like Gerald Dundas, it's that they don't take short cuts in life. Gerald is proof that if you find something you are passionate about, and then really put in the time to become a true genius at it, well then fame and fortune will eventually, and inevitably come your way. It's truly **inspirational**.

Like most geniuses I personally I *hate* short cuts. Despise them, really. I wouldn't light one on fire to stop another person pissing on it. But sometimes you have to do something you hate just to, you know, remind yourself of why you hate it, you know? So here goes, I am going to try out taking a short cut myself, this time on a story, that's right, this story.

Here we go:

It turned out the roommate ate the sandwich.

Oh **great**. *Just great.* I take a short cut and immediately I hit a *spoiler*. DAMMIT.

This was *clearly* going to be an awesome story. A totally enjoyable fun riddled ride. I can tell merely from the spoiler. Shit, this *would* have been a really *enjoyable* AND *entertaining* story!!!

Had I not taken that freakin' short cut we all could have had a great time. FUCK.

Based on the information in the line 'It turned out the roommate ate the sandwich' we can *clearly* declare that there was going to be at least TWO characters in this story, and we also know they were going to live together, because they were roommates. And stories with at least two characters ROCK. Plus at least two of them are roommates, like I pointed out, and oh my God roommates are *always* lots of fun, right?

And we've now missed out finding out if they were like a *crazy* messy one and an <u>uptight</u> clean one, which is like a history proven guide to *guaranteed* funny. Or perhaps it was going to be a flirtatious 'will they or wont they tale', which is *enthralling,* until they do 'it' (**'fuck'**) and it ruins everything, but did I mention that before that it will be *enthrawllilising*? It could have included all sorts of twisted and delightful things and we MISSED it. FUCKING hell, I LOVE finding out stuff about fictional roommates, stupid shortcut. Plus, **plus**, where was this room, ya know? Where? And we *missed* all that. Stupid *short cut*. AAAGHHH!

Oh and great, I just realized, this story was going to have a sandwich! Oh my God a Sandwich! And it's been eaten before I even found out what was *in* the sandwich. That changes SO much. Because if it was say a peanut butter sandwich I personally would have cared WAY more than if it was like some lame *turkey* sandwich, cause you know, I personally like peanut butter better than turkey, because peanut butter is delicious to people like me, by which I mean people who enjoy peanut butter. And now the story is ruined, and I don't even know if I should care or not about the sandwich? Damn **short cut**. ROOOOaaarrr.

Oh crap. So *now* it hits me, the line is 'it turns out the roommate ate' ect, you know the sandwich bit. 'Turns out'. That phrase is laden, positively **ladled** with mystery. Oh **no**, not 'he ate the sandwich', but 'IT TURNS OUT'. Fuck me in the bullet wound, there was going to be suspense and accusations, evidence, possibly clues, like crumbs or something, maybe questions unanswered until someone like answered them and all that, before an eventual SHOCKING 'turns out'.

This may have been expressed by someone with a line like '*oh my holy mother* **of God** it turns out the ROOMMATE ate the sandwich'! Which would have been awesome. Or someone could even have said 'shit, call the FBI immediately, things just got fucking *real*, it turns out the roommate' etc, you know ate the sandwich, which would have been high drama, or even cool ass sarcasm. Who knows anything? No one that's who, other than all of us, who *know* that we would have got some sort of REVEAL, of the **sandwich** being eaten. BLLLAAAUUGGGZZZZ. Cocksucking short cut.

So we'll never know, will we? The moment is destroyed like some planet we only JUST discovered, and then stepped on, because someone *had* to take a short cut.

I feel ashamed people. It was my experiment. My impatience. My fault. I ruined it. I ruined yet <u>another</u> fabulous sandwich mystery. And there can be no turning back. Oh no, once the sandwich is eaten it's done, it don't even matter if it's puked back up, it ain't comin' back up no God damn sandwich. By which I mean it would be like puke made up of sandwich bits, and there sure in **hell** ain't no fun mystery in regurgitated sandwich tales. The time has passed, and I take the blame.

But as *God* as my witness I shall never take a short cut........ again! (PS the use of those eight dots to signify a pause before the 'again' is the opposite of a short cut).

I am really upset. I think I am going to take a brief break from this book, but coming up soon – a story with a coffee table. Oh God damn it, was that a short cut *again*, grrrrrRRR, that better not be a spoiler, if anything 'turns out' in this story and it 'turns out' that the coffee table is part of that part of the story, I am seriously going to be mad.

Forty-Three

A lesson on how to sext

In this modern age there is one thing everyone should know how to do – send really creepy and over sexualized text messages to strangers, in vain, ill thought out and doomed to failure attempts to get laid. The problem is of course obvious, if you really want to creep someone out, then your standard dick pics and 'wanna fuck' type messages just don't offer enough bang for you text. Thankfully I have come up with a solution. Simply message the following to a stranger, and yes you still won't get laid, but you probably will at least successfully make their skin crawl:

I want to rip your clothes off
And pull you into me from behind
Fucking you in the ass… or similar
Deeper and harder and wider and squarer
Hearing you scream from every orifice
As you ponder the Tasmanian logging industry
My vodka infused natural lubricated knee caps
Will overcome every doubt in your loins
And in your moistest of brain juices
Like the aggregate of every bull whip sourced wound
And every wanna-be star gazing masturbation outsourcer
Like an orgy in a vat of duck fat sourced
organically so the ducks don't suffer
You'll be dripping with sweat

Ok, Intriguing: Hell Yeah! Awesomenessous

Like a Persian monkey on steroids
That turns out to be sitting on a coffee table
(Turns out? AGHHHHH!!)
And I want to catch every drop
In a bedpan that was already almost full
And watch you sponge bath yourself with it
Like a menopausal old woman in a nursing home
I'll be very near to you all day
But you won't lay a single eye on me
Because I'll be hiding
You don't know me
And yet you do
Because we already share the same STIs

It's as simple as writing that, and skin is a crawlin'. Of course you could also just say 'wanna come over and lick my scabs' – it's up to you.

Forty-Four

I'm here to protect you

I can tell by osmosis that many of my readers are big fans of the cops, some of you may even be thinking of calling the cops on me sometime soon because of perfectly innocent, and in some ways even generous text messages I have been sending you.

So I thought it was about time I mentioned that they won't do crap to help you, because I used to be one of them, and it might be time I talked about some of my days when I was a member of the boys in blue, the finest protectors in the world's little brother, the police force. (The finest protectors in the world are obviously surfers; their tireless, fearless, and salty efforts to protect us from sharks taking over the mainland should never be forgotten).

When I was a cop I was hard-core, that means I played by *my* rules, and my rules were neatly summed up in a book they gave us when we joined the police force. This book was referred to as 'the book' and if you decided, like me, to make your own rules fundamentally the same as the ones in 'the book' then your rules would be pretty much the same as everyone else's on the force, and that helped us all get along way better. Hell yeah, it's that kind of attitude which cops need to adhere to, or else beat partners get slapped by each other, and it's never manly for a man to slap another man (female police officers on the contrary are encouraged to slap their partners).

Now as a hard-core law enforcer one of my primary responsibilities was to go to schools to scare the kids straight by talking at their assemblies. (And by assembly I mean the assembilation of a group of kids, I was not talking while kids like assembled model air planes or something, no, never, not this cop).

These assemblies were always poorly attended of course. I guess the bad kids were always too scared to hear the truth! That's right, police uniforms are dry-clean only, so if you become a cop one day you need to take that into account or else the drain on your salary from keeping a clean uniform may severely throw off your projected spending power in the up-coming fiscal year. Those bad kids are always scared to hear someone say 'fiscal', I know it's hard to pronounce but that's no reason to flee the scene kids! I would often feel very guilty after these assemblies, but not for the bad kids lack of guts. No, for my own failures, but we'll get to that.

In these assemblies I'd get to say stuff like 'study hard or else they'll hold you back and make you repeat a year or two and then you'll end up that weird older guy still in school'.

'Hey, cop, aren't you like 30? *You're* the weird older guy in *this* school!' a kid would always inevitably yell out. And as the rest of the kids burst into laughter I would remember exactly why I decided to become a cop in the first place – to crack the skulls of smart-ass kids! So I would pull out my baton and charge at the kid ready to expose his cracked skull and show it off to the whole fucking school.

After the smart nerdy girls, who always sat up front, had tackled me, subdued me and kicked me out, I'd return to the police station and my sergeant would call me into his office

'Are you retarded?' he would yell at me.

'Well you were the one who hired me, you tell me?' I'd reply 'plus why get angry if you are posing that as a question, by definition a question should be something you are asking because you don't know the answer and therefore you should attach no emotion to it at all until the answer is forthcoming, which of course I have not provided, so there'.

Not wanting to own up to their own stupid decision-making when choosing a new employee to be part of their police squad these 'bosses', as we imaginatively called them, would usually remain quiet and I'd go unpunished.

This ability of mine to twist the facts and the realities to my own advantage was a key element of my police work.

'Case closed!' you would often hear me yell.

Of course I never actually had any cases. 'When you're a rogue cop who plays by your own rules which match up neatly against their rules then they don't give you cases' I would say to myself when I questioned why once again they were making me stay in the office and photocopy paper work I'd seen other cops pull from the trash after hearing a 'boss' say 'I don't know, just make up something for him to do'.

Still 'case closed' I would yell, because when I came to work I always packed a small suitcase in case I was sent out on undercover work, and I always packed light, so my suitcase was ALWAYS easy to get closed, none of that sitting on it bullshit you see so many disgraceful over-packers do all the time. 'Case closed' Hell Yeah it was, again and again and again.

That's why I often felt guilty after these assemblies. Because frequently I would be kicked out by the nerdy smart girls before I had the chance to tell the kids about the importance of not over packing.

'Pack light' I wanted to tell them kids 'because when they kick you out of somewhere and your bag is packed lightly, the people kicking you out are way less likely to think "this is pretty heavy, maybe we'll keep it in case it's full of valuables" and instead will chuck it at you while you lie on the grass with three twelve year old girls standing over you laughing!'

Is that an important lesson for the kids? Well *you* ask *me* – 'Is that an important lesson for the kids?' I hear you asking. Hell Yeah it is, 'case closed' you should imagine me saying, this time about the case of whether that is an important lesson for the kids or not rather than about closing my suitcase.

But you see I don't close cases any more. I have since been fired as a cop, and so no longer prepare myself for undercover work. Apparently somewhere in 'the book' it states that if you get kicked out of twenty seven school assemblies in one year then you get fired'. Personally, to be honest, as I cop I never actually read 'the book', I was too busy closing cases, practising how to pronounce 'fiscal' (I find thinking of it as two easy to pronounce words 'fiz' and 'cle' really helps you avoid any 'physical' embarrassments), but even without the knowledge of what is actually in this 'the book', there were very few murders on my watch, so are you welcome society? Case closed – yep!

Forty-Five

Hey, you know what, you're all pretty awesome

I know what you are thinking:

'This Dave fella is awesome, he's got a strange mind in the brilliant sense, and definitely NOT a strange mind in the "never ever be alone with him, I am sure he is carrying a knife, and why does he look at my kidneys like they are boobs" way and he never ever needs to boast or big note himself to overcompensate for his crippling insecurity, anxiety issues and life long struggles with severe clinical depression, being Dave must be awesome and that means it must be awesome to be someone else, oh man, I wish what I knew what it was like to be someone else, it must be awesome.'

Well I have ten things to say to you about this.

1. You think with long run on sentences, try using more punctuation in your thought process, if you don't know where to begin; try memorizing this book, because in this book the punctuation; spelling and use of grammar is floorless.
2. Little known fact: Floorless elevators are rarely flawless.
3. Yes, it *is* awesome to be Dave – I have severe insomnia so I am always up to date with what's happening on late night TV, very late night TV, very, very late night TV, and even very, very, very early morning TV, and very, very early morning TV. I get laid at least once every three years. I've just started a new diet and

exercise plan three days ago, so all this chub and lack of fitness will be something I embrace in two days when I quit my new diet and exercise plan. As I sit, writing this in a coffee shop, I just saw an asshole scream at someone a whole murder of insults for honking their car horn at him, something he could have easily avoided if he was willing to use his fucking indicator when trying to park his car, so I am not an asshole like him. I haven't had to update my prescription on my glasses in months. I am wearing a t-shirt with lots of drawings of cats on it, which is adorable. And it's been like three years since I've been laid, so I am due. Yep it's great to be Dave.

4. But no, it is NOT great to be someone else.
5. Your life is way better than you think it is.
6. You shouldn't wish to be someone else.
7. Because no it's NOT awesome to be someone else.
8. Yes I can prove it.
9. Shut up, I can so.
10. No *you're the* lying little loser! Then again, you sure do have sexy looking kidneys.

I have taken it upon myself to accurately guess just the type of people you covert being, rather than yourself, and I am going to show you just a little slice of their lives, on average routine days, going about their business, with nothing unusual for them going on at all.

What it's like to be a professionally trained antique glass blower upon showing up at your average dinner party:

'Hi Sonya, hi Heraldid, thanks for having me. I brought you guys these flowers, you know everyone brings wine, but why can't a guy bring his friends flowers, right? I'm *glad* you like them, yeah sure put them in a vase, that way we can all look at them while we're eating (smiles).

Oh you have a lovely home here, just lovely. These are your kids? Wow, they grow up fast don't they, not that I'd know, I never did get married and have kids, as you guys know. Wait this dinner isn't a cover for setting me up with one of your friends is it? Is it? Cause if it is I'd be fine with that, I guess you guys know I've been really lonely. Oh it's not. That's ok, no totally, I was just kidding around, being set up is HORRIBLE, much better to go out and find someone on your own.

Oh wow, is this painting a print or an original? Wow, original! I guess becoming a lawyer has paid off, huh Heraldid, good for you – go for the money, not the passion I always say, sure I love my craft, but it would be good to be able to pay the bills on time too, ha ha. Good for you Heraldid. You really have a nice house and family, you have it all, and you've invited me into your home for dinner, I feel honored to still be your friend, after all these years.

Oh those flowers look great in that vase, thanks Sonya. Woah woah, wait, hang on, is this a Folona vase? It is! This is a fucking Folona! Oh my God.

That's a fucking…. *factory* made vase!!!

How dare you? How dare you? Oh my God, you invite a professionally trained antique glass blower, like myself, to your house for dinner and have the meanness and down right cruelty to have him smell flowers, the ones that HE brought you, out of a *factory made* vase? Oh my God, how dare you?

Do you know how they make vases in factories, (he begins to wipe tears from his face) with machines! Yes fucking machines.

While people like me, good, nice, honest people, with talent in the beautiful art of antique glass blowing, go without a jobs in their chosen craft. How dare you? Oh my God. How DARE you?

I work in a mirror store for Christ's sake. You know that don't you? Do you know how heartbreaking that is to me? I sit at home every night blowing beautiful ornaments, vases, glasses, and I know people would love them, if people would just give them a chance, they would *love* them.

But then I come here and have to be reminded that even good people, my friends no less, keep generic, mass produced, job stealing factory made glassware in their house, and then have the audacity to put flowers in them, right in front of a wonderful artist in the beautiful art of traditional glass blowing.

I'm insulted, but more than that, I'm hurt, I am deeply hurt. I really feel betrayed, Heraldid, Sonya, you have betrayed me. I thought we were friends (begins sobbing).

Do you know what its like to turn on the TV and never see a hand crafted piece of glass anywhere? Even in wealthy upper class people's homes on TV. I'm sorry I don't buy someone living in a penthouse on Fifth Avenue New York filling their apartment with factory made glassware. It's just not fucking believable, these people like nice things, why would they not buy beautiful and unique hand crafted glassware. Why? I refuse to believe that.

Then again look at you, *oh my painting is an original, hand painted by the actual artist, not a factory made print, we like our art to be made by an artist* – except when it comes to fucking glassware, hey? So well maybe I can believe it, *but I don't like it*, I don't fucking like it one fucking bit!!

I don't want to live in a world where there is no love and respect given to hand crafted antique styled glassware, and I am sure as hell not staying around to eat dinner with the likes of you – you people epitomize the problem – because of YOU the world is a less pretty, less magical, less unique and full of bitter, lost, sad yet passionate, and honorable professionally trained antique glass blowers like myself who can't find a job in their chosen field because you'd rather support a fucking factory.

No Heraldid, it's not ok that I still have it as a hobby, hand blowing glass at home is really fucking expensive, it sucks up almost my entire wage, I can't pay my bills, my car needs new tires, I am fucking broke. You made me broke, YOU RUINED MY FUCKING LIFE.

Well I'm out of here. Go fuck yourself Heraldid. Go fuck yourself Sonya. I bet all your friends are ugly whores anyway, they must be to hang out with cunts like you who buy shitty factory made glassware even though they can clearly afford buy beautifully hand crafted.

Wait, unless you still could set me up with someone? That really would be great, I'm very lonely, and I can't meet a woman for some reason.

No? Please? (Really balling) No? Ok, fuck you, I never want to see you cunts again'.

What it's like to be an old school, old world, now grizzled, former Ford Factory worker brought back to talk to the current employees:

'Alright Ford staff, I am a former employee of this here factory, I worked the line here for over thirty years, and for all those years Ford was one the TOP companies in the world, and I have been brought in to talk to y'all about Ford's recent troubles.

First off I want to say (yelling) SIT UP AND SHUT THE FUCK UP. What the fuck is wrong with you people? People prefer Japanese cars now? Back in my day the only thing Japanese we preferred was a dead one on the end of your bayonet. And here I stand in front of the famous Detroit Ford Factory staff and I see a bunch of lazy, fat, dickheads, with little pride in their jobs, FORD *IS* AMERICA when YOU fuck up, you fuck up AMERICA! Japanese people are tiny little men, with tiny little dicks, who eat faggotty ass shit like sushi, and you're letting them beat you at the manliest profession there is, building cars? You people not currently eating a steak with your hands while saying to your fellow employees 'Suck my huge fucking cock' even though your dick is only average for an American, yet big compared Japanese cock IS FUCKING UP AMERICA!

'You there, slouchy, you're the CEO? (Screaming) How can you fuck up being CEO of the company that invented the factory line, sit the fuck up. Back in my day the CEO was the one who lugged the wheels from the truck, and after he'd done that he'd wipe grease on his shirt and make a joke about how if he was from Italy he'd come pre-greased up, then call the Italian guy working electronics a filthy pasta fucker "Hey do you stick the spaghetti up your ass before or after you cook it, you hairy greasy fuck" he'd yell. Mr CEO, your Italian suit and lack of stereotypical racial slurs aimed at the only minorities that we should let work here, being people who aren't quite white, yet still basically white is FUCKING UP AMERICA!

You, there, did I just see you yawn? (Really getting fucking loud) Is this boring to you, you work on the line right? Yeah you push a button now, in my day guys would work real machines, dangerous machines, and when they'd lose their hand, they'd go home with pride and say "I lost my hand for Ford", and when he came back to work, which would be the NEXT day, he'd then laugh when someone said "hey *hand* me a wrench" or "this is heavy, can you lend me a *hand*" or "I've got to *hand* it to you, even after your accident you still look *hand*some" and then he'd fish his severed hand out of the machine and go back to work. You people having two hands, and not setting up your fellow employees with simple jokes, where the punch line is at your expense and actually quite cruel makes me sick and you're FUCKING UP AMERICA!

You there, the young lady (roaring with hellfire in his eyes) What the HELL are you doing even being in this fucking room? Shouldn't you be at home playing with cats? Back in my day women only came into the Ford Factory when we hired strippers for peoples birthdays, and then she'd end up fucking a bunch of guys because that meant she could say she fucked a Ford man. You being in this room and doing anything other than sliding up and down a poll while taking a long time to take off your panties even though we don't give a shit about anything you are doing until those fucking panties are off, and then taking the young bloke who's still a virgin and fucking him behind the compactor, before coming out holding up his hand like he's just won a prize fight, before saying loudly 'he was almost all the way inside me before he came' waiting for a laugh and then saying 'now where's a real Ford man willing to fuck me properly' and when fifty four hands go up then responding with 'this is going to be a long fun afternoon' is FUCKING UP AMERICA!

Which actually reminds me, I've now got to go head over to the Barbie Doll factory – do you know they are now building some dolls that don't present an image of unrealistic beauty guaranteed to make all young ladies dedicate their lives to looking unhealthily skinny and blonde with big fake tits? HOLY SHIT are *THEY* FUCKING UP AMERICA!

What it's like to be a crazy cat lady who also happens to be a staunch vegan:

'Miss Snuggle Puss, come over here and have a seat please, we need to have a talk.

I don't know how to start, but I guess I should just tell you what's going on. I found them, I found the feathers, oh my, yes Miss Snuggle Puss, I found the *feathers*.

(Mortified) It's happened hasn't it? That adorable little kitten I adopted two years ago has made the change. You're a *muuuurderer* now.

How many times have I told you? Eating meat is murder. Eating meat is MURDER. Miss Snuggle Puss, I told you, I told you, I told you over and over, eating meat is MURDER, it's MUUUURRRDDDEEERRRR!!!! So why did you do it? Why did you become a *muuuurrrddeerrrer*?

How long has this been going on Miss Snuggle Puss, tell me? How many lives have you taken? How many species? Birds, rodents, what else, don't tell me fish, please don't tell me fish, no body should ever, EVER eat fish? Please don't tell me you muuuurder fish?

(Wounded) Oh I don't know what to do, I love you, I do love you Miss Snuggle Puss. But you're a murderer now, you are now no better than those monsters you see on the news like serial killers, and genocidal dictators, and people who eat at Sizzler. Do you deserve to go to lethal injection? Probably. But no, no, no I could never do that to you, and that would make me a killer, just like you have become. Oh no Miss Snuggle Puss, look at the position you have put me in. I love you, but you have the taste for muuuurder now, and I cannot let that continue, I cannot allow this house to be a house of *mmuuuurrrddeeerrr*.

(Ashamed) I've tried to protect you from this, I tried to keep you inside away from temptation, sure you could see birds out the window, but I thought you'd learn to appreciate them for their pretty feathers, and amazing ability to master the art of flight, I never thought you'd look at them and think 'I should murder that'. Oh my, I failed, I failed myself and I failed you, because seeing birds, and even imagining horrible things, is still very different from chasing, and killing and slaaauuughtering, how can I ever trust a *muuuuurderer* again?

Maybe I do have to kill you to stop you, but I have been down that path with so many former kitties of mine, and I cannot, oh Miss Snuggle Puss, you have hurt me so bad. You're making me think that cats don't even want to be vegans. That in fact cats have murder deep down in their DNA, but that can't be true can it, I love cats, can you all be *muuuurrrdddeerrrs*? In fact after you I might stop even getting cats, is that what you want me to do? I guess it is. I stopped eating meat because I didn't want to be a murderer, and I must hold you to the same standards as I hold to myself.

(Devastated) This is going to hurt me more than it hurts you (snaps Miss Snuggle Puss's neck), see Miss Snuggle Puss, see what it's like to be *muuuuurrrddeerredddd*? You didn't like it did you.

You know what, maybe I'll get a bunny for my next pet. Yes bunnies aren't muuurrrdddeeerrs. That'll work.

(Chucks Miss Snuggle Puss in the trash).

So now do you see people? Being someone else isn't that great. If you were someone else, just think of the horrible, despicable and disgusting things that would be true about you. You'd:

- Be a bad dinner guest.
- Have friends with bizarre names, names like 'Sonya'.
- Be a lonely loser who is desperate for his friends to set him up on dates, but they still don't.
- Use horrible words like the 'c' word (cunt).
- Be great at loss-of-appendage based puns.
- Have a slight temper problem, and possibly even a slight bit of racism or even chauvinism.
- Think America is being fucked up.

- Be a man who cares about Barbie Dolls.
- Not be as nice to adorable little kitties as they deserve.
- Elongate words, even words like murder.
- Have a pet bunny instead of an awesome pet, like a kitty.

So you're feeling better about yourself now aren't you? Yay. So are you welcome society? Case closed – yep!

Forty-Six

How your life is at risk from a newly discovered yet very common disease

If you are like me, you are still a bit pissed off at the guy from the previous chapter who got pissed off at people honking their car horns at him even though he was the one who didn't use his indicator. What a fucking asshole, just a mere mention of this fuckwad is, I am sure, making every single one of you throb with rage, and wanting to whip him in the face with some form of crudely home made sword, until there is nothing left standing but a neck where a head used to be, and a floor covered in humorously arranged face parts. Now, while yeah sure, making a Picassoesq painting of his face on the floor using his actual face parts does sound on the surface both cool and well deserved, but as I am going to now expose, I think just perhaps some of you are being a tad harsh.

I don't like to get too political, plugged in or socially aware in my life, but this week I have been given access to some exclusive scientific research about a very real disease that the man above, and even you, may currently unknowingly be suffering from, and at the very least are definitely at risk of being a victim of. Yes, this is a very serious disease. This disease may very well be putting your life, and the lives of all the people you know, and love in danger every single day, including today, yesterday and even tomorrow.

You may be at risk from dying as a result of this disease this very minute. You may even already be dead. You may currently be reading this in the afterlife wondering, 'why was nothing done to stop this, why did I never even hear of this before, and why did I have to wait to get to the judgment hall waiting room before getting to read a book as awesome as this?' I am talking, of course, about a horrible disease known simply as 'LSB'.

'LSB' or 'Lazy Scum-Bag' is a condition that scientists have only just recently discovered, and is thought to possibly be the root of why so many vehicle, motorcar and automobile drivers seem unable or unwilling to use their car's 'indicator', 'blinker' or as suffers call them 'why do they have that weird stick next to my steering wheel in every car I drive?'

Sorrow riddled sufferers of LSB have been seen across the world failing to indicate while doing the following:

- Turning left.
- Turning right.
- Changing lanes.
- Parking.
- Trying to hit dogs.
- Exiting driveways.
- Trying to hit cats.

Sound ghastly? It is, but here is where it gets extraordinarily scary - LSB's have be known to fail to indicate even when there are other cars around that need to know the LSB's plans before navigating their own situation in the safest way possible, when pedestrians are in the vicinity possibly about to walk exactly where LSB's are planning to turn under a cloak of false safety from the car lights suggesting it is planning on going straight and not turning at all, and yes, *even when* there is no one around but they are still legally required to use their blinking tool!

Good…. GOD.

This despite activating said indicator requiring nothing more than moving a finger two inches from where it already is, or should be!

Every day more and more people develop the symptoms suggesting the early stages of LSB, and once it takes hold, life, as they know it, is nothing but hell. As one long suffer of LSB described the ordeal of his horrible affliction:

'Using my blinker requires me to move my finger two inches! Fuck that, I'd much rather kill a kid!'

LSB has been noticed by experts for many years but always discounted as not being a real condition due to sufferers often simultaneously partaking in activities that are dangerous and/or annoying despite in *these* cases it requiring MORE effort than treating their fellow drivers with respect.

Activities like:

- Honking their horn at someone for doing something they themselves often do guilt free.
- Tailgating despite the car in front already going the speed limit and the fact tailgating is most likely to slow them down now that they have been put in danger.
- Not kindly allowing someone into your lane, and then giving them the finger when you force them to force their way in.

For years experts have thought these activities were merely caused by people being 'selfish' and/or being 'total assholes' mostly because these people are also those things. That's why LSB caught scientists so off guard, because in terms of effort, it is in direct opposition to the regular behavior of the LSB. One expert was recently quoted saying:

'Turns out even total assholes are capable of getting diseases, wow we're in luck, maybe they'll also get Hodgkin's Luphoma, that's a real thing right?'

If you are a sufferer of LSB not all hope is lost. Help is out there, counseling can help, losing your license for a DUI has been known to minimize the regularity of outbreaks and there are also full cures, such as:

- Jumping off a high balcony.
- Putting your head in the oven and slow roasting it like beef brisket.
- Going to a hospital and seeing a crippled brain damaged kid who was hit by a car that didn't indicate, and then explaining to his parents exactly why moving your finger two inches is too hard.
- Getting blinded by shards of glass after crashing into a kitchen appliance store.
- Thinking to yourself 'I'm a dangerous fucking douche bag, is this how I was raised?' And answering 'Yes, it was, I guess it's time for a parental/self murder suicide'.
- Taking taxis (please note most taxi drivers themselves suffer from LSB).

If a slower approach is more your style you can also simply start moving your finger two inches occasionally and try to build on it, and in the meantime hope to only kill something small, like a puppy, rather than a kid. If you're not ready to try moving your finger two inches in a driving situation you can also start at home, you'll find all sorts of benefits, cans of beer can now not just be held but also opened, TV channels can be changed with a remote, and you can point at things and say to someone exciting things like 'was that pot plant always there?'

Sadly of course, most LSB suffers will never seek help as one of the symptoms of LSB is a condition known as 'LYNDAW' or 'Like You've

Never Done Anything Wrong' which is a weird tick like response LSB sufferers will spew once having it pointed out that moving ones finger two inches is not that big an ask seeing as it saves lives.

'Like you've never done anything wrong!' They'll yell.

Yes sadly, in the LSB mind, the fact that there are few flawless humans in the world justifies anything they may do wrong themselves, despite how possibly catastrophic the result may be and the clearly available simple solution.

So sad.

So if you meet a LSB sufferer give them a hug, they're suffering, then tackle them to the ground and steal their car keys, just because they're diseased doesn't mean they should be allowed to kill us.

Forty-Seven

This week on The Real Housewives of Saudi-Arabia

'What do you mean your tennis coach saw your cheek?'

'It was an accident I swear, there was a big gust of wind that blew my headscarf slightly off my cheek, it was just for a fleeting moment'.

'Fuck you, you bitch whore, get outside so I can stone you to death'.

'No please poppa, no, it was a really big gust of wind, Sally got caught in it too, I saw her socks, if she wasn't wearing any, her ankles would have been exposed, it was definitely a really big gust!'

'You saw another girls socks too! Ok what's Sally's fathers number, I am sure he'll need me to rape her, now why are you inside still, get outside now, you know insubordination is a stoneable offense too, and I can't stone you to death twice, what are you trying to do, have Allah hate me?'

Next week on the real housewives of Saudi-Arabia find out which of your favourite housewives daughters gets gang raped and killed, and then has her head stuck on a spear next to a bridge by her brothers as a warning, after it was discovered that a boy had had an impure thought about her.

Forty-Eight

Coming soon To a TV near you - possibly even in FRONT of you

Fanatical religious beliefs of any kind, anywhere, which oppress women and children, or anyone for that matter, are of course no laughing matter. Having said that, if the previous chapter taught us anything, and it did, it's that once my wildly original TV show idea 'The Real House Wives of Saudi Arabia' is picked up and takes off, it will change the way we see our television entertainment. Television will be on a new path, a journey if you will, to a better place. A place where we no longer rely on heavily scripted 'reality TV', and shows based around shock tactics, but instead get down to the real honest truth. Television that does not merely entertain, but inspires, enlightens and educates. This excites me.

As the man likely to be charged with being the founding father of a new era, I am sure all eyes will be on me to see what else I have up my haphazardly scrunched up sleeves. So you will, I am sure, all be relieved to know that I have countless more brilliant ideas hiding up there. And I am now going to give you exclusive access to these concepts, so you can all call your friends in the entertainment industry, and send them my way, and we can get this new era of Hell Yeah awesomenessous TV upon us as soon as possible.

Sitcoms

Couwffee..... or irony? - A guy opens a coffee shop in an ethnically diverse neighborhood and finds imitating the various accents of his customers endlessly fun... until he gets stabbed. After six months in the hospital, upon discharge, he's told to 'lay off the caffeine' the very stuff he's got to sell to pay his medical bills!

You think you've got it bad - After a psychiatrist discovers a cluster of his former clients have gone on to commit suicide he has a mental breakdown leaving him literally unable to say anything other than a sarcastically toned *'you think YOU got it bad?'* And to his surprise he's now able to REALLY help those in need, but can he help himself? No, not really.

Climbing women - A gang of recreational rock climbing women find climbing the male dominated corporate ladder is not as easy as cliffs - especially as they're all (dum dum dum) women! Will they be 'roped' into bad deals, will they occasionally 'abseil' into the odd conference call, will they 'figure eight knot' the man of their dreams? Or will their 'webolette, piton catchers and thrutching' get in the way? Stay tuned!

Dramas

Thick Marker - In a world where there is a fine line between pleasure and pain, truth and lies, and love and hate - a man who runs a small failing stationary shop is really frustrated he isn't selling more thick markers.

Men in heat? – An gaggle of men who lack a lot of patience are sent to a different sauna every week to try and relax, but will their lack of patience allow them to hang around until those coals actually get hot? Who knows?

My incest freak baby – After a particularly awesome first date a teenage boy discovers that the girl he just slept with is his sister who had run away from home six months ago and got a haircut. Now they are pregnant with an incest freak baby, but much to their surprise raising a very, very special need baby in the modern world with no money, no skills, no help from their horrified parents, and no idea how to change a diaper on a three ass cheeked kid, is slightly harder than they first imagined. Will their relationship survive? Will they ever get used to having their house egged? Will their kid decide to have its penis removed or its vagina sewed up, or (dum dum dum) – KEEP BOTH? This is listed in drama, but is clearly more of a dramady.

Animal documentary

Putting spiders in fires - a show where we take a type of creature, a spider for example, and throw the fucker in a fire. The highlights would be when the fire burns the spiders.

Reality shows

Retards in a pit - A show where we put severely mentally challenged people in a pit, and see how long it takes them to get out. It should be a pit that would be easy to get out of if you are not mentally challenged. This one would definitely play with a laugh track.

Sidney needs a Kidney. We find people who are in desperate need of kidney transplants and pair them with naive poor teenagers who think it would be totally worth giving up a kidney for an Ipad. Contestants named Sidney will be given priority.

The perfect mother for the father - a single man who wants a wife and baby is set up with thirty women, whom we now impregnate with his sperm. Each week he must ask the girl he likes the least to leave the house and abort his child, till he is left with his perfect partner - and a perfect family is born.

The test - a staunch pro-lifer is kidnapped and impregnated with sperm taken from a non-white, extremely low IQ, convicted sex offender - will she stay pro-life, switch sides or merely 'accidentally' fall down the stairs?

Abort or not, we let pop culture morons decide. We find pregnant twelve year olds and have them compete against whoever's the current 'famous for nothing other than being a pretentious superficial moron' celebrity in a series of tests of intelligence, creativity and percentage of body filled with Botox, if you can't beat them in absolutely every category then you are deemed clearly too stupid to raise a child and get your foetus aborted live on camera. If you do beat them all, then the pop culture moron decides if you keep the baby or not. Clause 1: you must have *specifically* gotten pregnant in hope of getting on the show. Clause 2: MTV is not responsible for the fact we are clearly responsible for encouraging you to ruin your life, and that of your potential kid. Clause 3: If you get pregnant to an immediate family member and it is decided that you must keep your baby, then we want your kid to audition to play the freak baby in our dramedy 'My incest freak baby'.

These last three are of course all part of our new hot Thursday line up - **Must see abortee TV**. To be immediately followed by:

The count – A bunch of fertility experts, without ever seeing the contestants, or even hearing them sing – test a sample of their sperm for sperm count and sperm quality, the higher the count and quality, the faster the men get to get their vasectomy, all of whom are desperate for them, seeing as they are currently in sexual relationships with immediate family members and have watched at least ten minutes of my incest freak baby.

You're welcome TV fans!!! Thanks to me, television is about to escape the dark path it is currently on towards an epic dumbing down of society and/or higher and higher staked shock tactics, and will instead get more intelligent, more original, more thought provoking, more inspirational, clearly funnier and without a doubt more entertaining. People will probably start watching so much TV that sales of books may even go down a small tiny amount. Woah, lucky I switched from writing books to TV just in time.

Still, I am not finished with my awesomenessous generosity yet. Oh no, not this guy. I am even willing to volunteer my services to star in and/or host any or all these shows. This generous offer includes the following promises:

- Brilliant acting.
- Hilarious joke delivery.
- Tear jerking dramatic performances.
- Huge energy hosting skills.
- A willingness to humiliate myself in just about anyway (please see my episode of 'Dating in the Dark' for proof) and last but definitely not least.
- Puns. Yes! PUNS!

'Welcome to Sidney needs a kidney, because sometimes your new kidney is more than a.... *stones*... throw away. This next retard spent so much time stuck in a pit she has a ..... *hole*... lot of problems. Will John keep Stephanie around for another week with a chance to be his "perfect mother" or will this rose ceremony really, really, really... *suck*'.

You're welcome television fans.

Forty-Nine

I think it's time carpet got more respect, WAY more respect

Let's just be honest right up the top here, carpet deserves way more respect, WAY more respect. The thing about carpet is that it that is better than a cardboard cut-out of a bucket of sand, right? And people just don't think about that anywhere near enough.

I mean think about it, a cardboard cut-out of a bucket of sand is pretty freaking useless. Unless of course you are entering a cardboard cut-out of a bucket of sand competition; and then ok, I'm willing to admit that even a really soft, pure, plush carpet made with premium Marino wool will win you few points in a cardboard cut-out of a bucket of sand competition, but be honest with yourself, how often are you going to enter a cardboard cut-out of a bucket of sand competition? Two, maybe three times a month? At least. But how often are you going to walk on your carpet? Probably daily!

Outside of the professional circuit, cardboard cut-outs in general are pretty useless to be quite frank. They are poor alternatives to the real thing. Like have you seen those cardboard cut-outs of celebrities? What can you do with them? Just look at em and stuff. Plus buckets of sand don't do much for you, I mean you're at the beach, there is sand freaking everywhere, why put it in a bucket? To steal! And that's not nice. So you'd have to be insane to choose a cardboard cut-out of a bucket of sand over having your house carpeted.

And think about this, maybe you want to tell a friend that you are going to have an abortion but you don't know how to say it, so you're looking for a metaphor you can use which will be easy to act out and will clearly get your point across without you needing to say the actual word 'abortion', what are you going to do? It's obvious isn't it, you will put a small pile of sand (proving you had an *actual* bucket of sand, so cardboard cut-out, are you fucked in the head?) on the carpet, tell your friend you are pregnant, then say 'but hey see that sand, imagine for a moment that's my fetus', then you will grab your vacuum cleaner and vacuum the sand up. Your friend will hug you, and say 'I support your decision', and it will never be spoken about again. But try that without carpet and see what happens, 'I don't get it, why did you vacuum your hard wood floors, isn't it easier to use a broom, and oh my God YOU'RE PREGNANT, YOU'RE GOING TO BE A GREAT MOM!!!!' and now because the word 'mom' has been used you suddenly get all emotional and you end up raising a child you didn't want, all because you didn't have carpet!!!!

That's insane, a life long commitment because you had no carpet? Oh my God. Get a carpet you psycho.

But carpet isn't great just when comparing it to situations involving either cardboard cut-outs of buckets of sand and/ or real actual sand. Carpet is great just on its own. Check out this true story – when I was a kid my house had pea green shag carpeting. After a time we didn't like this type of carpet anymore, because it looked really ugly and was good at hiding spiders, so we ripped it up and put in new carpet, and for some reason some family friends wanted this old shag carpet full of spiders and so we gave it to them and they carpeted their floor with this carpet. Years later shag carpet kind of became retro cool, and one of the kids in that house ended up playing many, many Rugby games for the Australian Rugby Union team, the Wallabies, including playing in several World Cups! Yep that's right, pea green shag carpet spiders can give you Rugby playing super powers!!! Wow. And you're going to choose a cardboard cut-out of a bucket of sand instead? You'll make your high school B Rugby team at best. Are you mad?

Still not convinced? Well check out these reasons why having carpet is awesome:

1. It is soft under your feet, which is nice and stuff.
2. If you invite people over to your house, and you don't have very interesting artwork on the walls, hand blown glassware on the mantle, or a nice view from the windows your guests will be able to say 'I like your home, nice carpet'.
3. Carpet comes in a variety of styles and designs; that puts YOU in control, not your floor.
4. If you are prone to randomly fainting, and your home is carpeted, you're less likely to crack your head open when you fall (unless you keep low tables all over the place, but really if you're prone to fainting just don't do this, it would be nuts).
5. Door to door carpet cleaners are usually great conversationalists, because they do it all day, so they are well trained.
6. Some people refer to a ladies vaginal region by referencing carpet when the lady does not have vigilant grooming practices and when this comes up in conversation, perhaps in the bar or around a lively game of scrabble, you'll be able to think of her vagina and think of your carpet at home, and just smile warmly.
7. Some men refer to their chest hair as their carpet, if they are like really hairy, which lets you know how hairy a guy is often before you have even seen him shirtless, and you know, as they say 'knowledge is power', which isn't true because power is power not knowledge, you can even look that up in a dictionary under definitions of words, but still people say that, so it'll be nice to have that knowledge.
8. If you are ever murdered the offenders hair and skin fragments are more likely to be found and DNA tested in a carpeted house, because carpet is a great magnet for hair and skin fragment, so straight up, carpet catches killers earlier in their killing career,

which means carpet = life saving. Think about it, if the person the killer killed one before you had carpet, YOU might be ALIVE right now, oh my God, now don't you want everyone to have carpet?

9. If you ever get really, really hungry you can eat carpet, it won't taste nice, be easy to eat, satisfy your hunger, or have any positive affect what so ever, but it's nice to have options right?

10. Even some poor people have carpet; do you really want *those* people to have something over you?

11. If you have kids who spill drinks a lot, when one of them starts drinking a drink while standing on the carpet you get the chance to yell 'not on the carpet!'

The point is:

So do you have a carpet, if not why the hell not?

Do you ever think 'dude humans eat salad and that's like leaves what are we rabbits?' And then you realize, seriously dude you're still saying 'dude'?

When you get called the life of the party do you freak out, cause if you're the 'life' what the hell are these other people, zombies, ghosts, shit loads of ants in human skin outfits? Holy fuck ants must have *won* that war over crumbs.

Do you ever go to a party, stand in the middle of the room, start eating a Snickers Bar and then go 'mmm mmmmm mmmm this tastes so good it's like there's a party in my immediate surroundings'?

Well Fun Fact: Parties sometimes take place on carpet!!!!!!!!!!!!!

Fifty

Speaking of friendship

Stephanie was there today. I'd met her a long time earlier when she was selling plastic owls at a plastic owl shop on a day I that was shopping for plastic owls.

Her shop didn't have any plastic owls that met my plastic owl needs that day so I promised I'd come back. A promise I kept every day for years.

This impressed Stephanie. 'I'm impressed by a man who is clear and dedicated to his specific plastic owl needs' she said to me, on my 754th straight day coming into the plastic owl store and failing to find a plastic owl that fit my plastic owl needs. 'I like a girl who sells plastic owls' I replied. And we've been friends ever since. We can talk for hours - about owls, about plastic, sometimes even about plastic owls!

It was from her that I discovered that sometimes they use plastic to make birds *other* than owls, such as eagles, hawks, tits, salamanders, pigeons, koalas, canaries, condors and even some non-predatory birds! Quite incredible really. Can you imagine that? A plastic pigeon? Wow.

It was also from her that I found out that plastic owls are mostly used to discourage birds, such as geese, ostriches, penguins, kiwis, budgies, platypus, dwarf cassowaries, and even some non-non-flightless birds, from landing on your balcony, because they are scared that the plastic owl will eat them, which can save that area being contaminated with bird poop! Quite incredible really. Can you imagine that? A plastic owl eating a penguin? Wow.

I was glad to see Stephanie today as I'd recently stopped visiting the plastic owl store. You see I shockingly discovered, after doing some research into a topic that had not made it into one of our chats about plastic owls, much to my utter astonishment, that beavers can't climb apartment buildings. I know! So I no longer even needed a beaver scaring plastic owl. I learned four other important things that day too:

1. The reason why Stephanie's plastic owl store never had a plastic owl that suited my plastic owl needs.
2. The reason why the toothpick collection I keep on my fifteenth floor balcony has never been stolen by beavers.
3. That even Stephanie, who has worked in the plastic owl business for years, still has some gaps in her plastic owl knowledge.
4. And that an example of Stephanie's gap in knowledge about plastic owls would be the fact that beavers cannot climb apartment blocks.

I was really looking forward to seeing Stephanie because I knew she'd be excited about expanding her plastic owl knowledge, but here is the thing, we had so many other things to talk about today that I never got around to it!

Like for example, during our chat, I learned that plastic can be used to make animals that aren't even birds at all! Like alligators, lions, silver back gorillas, bar-tailed godwits, kitties, owls, camels, grizzly bears and even non-non-predatory-non-bird-animals! Quite incredible really. Can you imagine that? A plastic camel that doesn't eat pigeons? Think of all the poop you'd get on your balcony!

Friendship sure is awesome. Wow.

Fifty-One

The new normal

I think what we have proven over the past fifty odd ('fifty' to be precise. Of course that does also fit precisely into the description 'fifty odd', if you want a whole deferent type of precise) chapters, is that, man life is pretty normal for most people. It's just normal this, normal that, sometimes even normal there – well screw that, I want to be normal sure, but not in the normal ways, no sir. In fact I am of the belief that I am SO normal that I have been given an important task, and I am going to grasp it – that's right I am going to take normal to places it's never ever been before!

I am going to strap a backpack to normal, point it north and tell it not to come back till it's seen things that has blown its eyes right out of its sockets, so that they are left hanging and bouncing around on its chest like a tiny kangaroo boxing it, only to look down and realize its eyes are actually looking into cave filled with super clean breakfast plates, yeah that's right normal!

I am going to lock normal in a basement and tell it that when it comes up its body may well be covered in random bruises but that's nothing compared to the bruises it will feel on its mind, and not just any part of its mind, but the parts that have never been used before, the parts full of donuts made out of elephant dreams, the parts where people sexually moan about dust on lampshades, the parts where 'two plus two clingy grouper filling' makes more sense than anything that's ever come out of the ear of a gnat, yeah that's right normal!

I'm going to cover normal in honey then throw it out of a moving space train that's been lost in the amazon jungle, and when it looks up and finds the honey is being licked off it will discover the tongues of Mayan pyramids ravishing it in an orgy of over conditioned confidence issues mixed with self perpetuating terrible arrogance, only the tongues won't be made of flesh, but of the soft smell of rain washing away a single beer burp, yeah that's right normal!

I'm taking you on a journey normal, so be scared, be afraid, be wounded like the only cloud on a sunny day that is shaped like a giant guitar in the sky only with no one to play it, so you start to fall apart into random vapor that will drift into a champagne flute, however when you go to take a sip you'll find that there is a huge shard missing from the side of the glass, but how is the orange juice it's filled with not falling it out? How? HOW? Yeah that's right normal, be afraid, you have now met David Tieck, and life is going to be very different for you from now on, I am going to fuck you up normal. I am going to take you places you can't even imagine. Your days of boring the fuck out of us all are done.

Oh also, normal, are any of those super clean breakfast plates you have there actually cereal bowls? I'm gonna go ahead and eat some cereal right now, but get this; it's currently dinnertime! Suck on that normal.

Fifty-Two

And now signs that the bottom of your cannon may need a scrub

I know what you're thinking, 'I own an awesome cannon, but how do I know if the bottom may need a scrub?'

Fear not, my fellow cannon owners, by which I assume I mean all of you - here are some very simple signs that have the ability to signify to you that it is time to get down and scrub that beautiful cannon bottom of yours:

- It's a really old cannon.
- Your cannon was a gift from a new foe, who *was* a former friend, until you discovered that all his gifts had a part of them that needed scrubbing.
- Your cannon is currently half submerged in a mud-rat riddled swamp.
- You're a not currently a clean freak.
- You've never sworn your allegiance to the master of the under cleaners, by which I mean you tip your maids poorly.
- You have a filthy mind, and your cannon is imaginary ha ha, like anyone has a dirty mind and yet doesn't have a real cannon.
- You like to bounce dirty balls on the floor in your cannon room.

- You're a believer of the phrase 'smile at a partridge, smell a brown sided tree, never meet a bald witch, and the bottom of your cannon probably needs a scrub' and you've been smiling and smelling when you should have been meeting.
- The rest of your cannon needs a scrub - I mean who ONLY scrubs the bottom?
- The bottom of your cannon looks dirty.

How did you all fair? Ya scrubbing or not? I'm not, my cannon is spotless. I HAVE sworn an allegiance to the master of the under cleaners, that's right she's real! So you better start tipping your maids right you bastards!

Fifty-Three

I hope you brushed your teeth

Oh no, we're coming at a very fast speed, depending on your reading skills, towards something very, very sad - the end of this book. I'm sorry, this is clearly affecting you very hard, and it's not just you either, this is a very sad moment for all of us, even me. This may even be the saddest moment ever for some of you, at least those among you who are assholes that have never had to deal with the types of true suffering you only know if you've survived a war, watched loved ones die, agonized through severe illness or depression, lived in poverty, or dated an average female (zing). Yes life has been tough for some, and if coming to the end of this book isn't the saddest, hardest, and wettest thing you have ever faced, well then you have my sympathy, and empathy, I always forget which is which, so I make sure to offer both.

Still, regardless of your life up till now, riddled with horror, or perfect up until this very moment, this book ending is sure to make you sad right now. This is not my mission however. No, I am not here to make you sad, that is neither my job nor my intention. In fact, contrary to that, I am I'm here with one goal in mind - to make you smile. And let's be honest, I am pretty bloody good at it, I bet which ever big name celebrity I decide upon to write my foreword will probably even rave about my ability to make people smile. It is simply in my nature, I don't need to boast about it, or shove it in people's faces. I leave that up to other people. Instead I just *see* it on people's faces, especially during

178

the precise moments that they are in the present process of smiling because of me, which I get to enjoy at least annually, sometimes even bi-annually!

Well, and this is pretty impressive, but frankly I am about to outdo even my own expectations right here, and in fact before we sail off into the sad, sad sunset, I'm first going to give you barrage, no no a stampede, make that a blitz, or a tsunami, a firing squad, or a violent murder spree, a God damn genocidal rampage or dare I say it even a *LIST* of reasons for you to smile:

- Smile because of butterflies, which are way better than God's first attempt 'Margarine Wasps'.
- Smile because of the beverage that is presently in my mouth, as it finally fulfills its preordained destiny, which gives hope that you too may some day end up in my mouth.
- Smile if you find enjoyment in the playing of a guitar, which is one of the best signs out there that there is a chance you are not addicted to porking teddy bears.
- Smile because of mosquitoes, because if you grind up a shit load of them in a jar they make an excellent alternative to jam on an English muffin.
- Smile if you're an alcoholic, as unlike other people, you can regularly enjoy naps in other people's gardens.
- Smile for 'out of a scale of 1-10', for including just about everyone, except the REAL ugos.
- Smile because of the existence of minor headaches, for being an awesome excuse to complain, without the horror of actual discomfort.
- Smile for the word 'trout', for being the most fun word to scream in the mouth of a hungry bear.
- Smile for jokes that require a bit of a reach in logic, ha ha magnetic squirrels stealing buses! Brilliant!

- Smile because of organic catfish, for being equally as good as catfish bred using pesticides, not like some foods that are always disappointing when organic, such as organic spaceships.
- Smile because of geniuses, for actually getting shit done, not like those lazy bastards Genies.
- Smile for every time I've stayed home all week crafting a love song for my lady, and in doing so letting her know that I'd rather stay home and write songs than be with her.
- Smile because of the word 'Boing', and for it only getting more and more awesome no matter how many extra Os you add - 'Boooooooooooooinng'.
- Smile if you're hoping to chase self-improvement, for being far more achievable than *my* personal goal of 'stealth' improvement.
- Smile for 'mid sized sedans' for being a way cooler term than the original 'giant sized misshaped small trunked family friendly mini vans'.
- Smile for the ability to add 'man' to the end of sentences, finally offering a way for kids to progressively mature away from ending sentences with 'dude'.
- Smile for sharp knives, for being way better dinner companions than trampoline buddies. And finally
- Smile for the existence of a 'center of attention', something that is laughingly easy to become, just as long as you're willing to permanently staple an aardvark to your face.

Aren't smiles awesome! Sometimes I even try to do it myself, occasionally even TRI-annually!

Fifty-Four

Some parting advice

Now, I know what you're thinking:

'This book is nearly over, and even though I just can't stop smiling about all the enjoyment I've enjoyed, what am I going to do for fun next, keeping in mind the expensive cost of living in this highly gadget heavy time, while also being mindful of an economy that is fragile and untrustworthy? I just wish I had advice on something, that is reliably fun to do, which requires very little set up time or effort, and is cheap enough to do just about any day, and on even the slimmest of budgets?'

Well as usual, dearest readers, I have not merely just entertained you for this past two hundred to seven hundred odd pages, but I have also got your future entertainment high on my list of priorities.

The following is something you can do for a reliably, Hell Yeah, awesomenessous good time, for practically no money, and get this, it's also a great hang over cure. This game is called:

Photo Finish

Step One: Go to a your nearest mall, and head over into the food court during the busiest time they have.

Step Two: Pull up a seat in the middle of all the activity, and while making as much of a scene as you can, slowly open a can of dog food and begin eating it with a fork.

Step Three: As you consume the can of dog food, really, really make sure everyone knows that you are seriously enjoying it. Sell your enjoyment with 'mmmmms' and almost orgasmic moans and groans, and out loud declarations like 'this is seriously delicious', and if you want to get crazy, feel free to even add in a 'yuuuumm'!

Step Four: Now, and this is where it really gets fun, as soon as people clearly start looking a bit sick, and maybe even stop eating the food they were enjoying only moments before, and start looking at you instead, suddenly yell out: 'this is the *best* dog food I have ever eaten, YOU CAN REALLY TASTE THE HORSE!!!!!'

Now, I know what you're thinking:

'There is a flaw in your game David, a challenge *you* may not even see, just one little element about this which I am not sure I can justify, or get my head around, it's just that sometimes tin cans can be hard to open and create sharp edges which you can easily cut yourself on, and cutting myself might severely dampen my Hell Yeah awesomenessous fun. Especially if there is blood, ew gross, blood?'

Well my good readers, yes, blood is gross, but ha ha, not to worry at all, at your local kitchen appliance store you will find a myriad of fancy modern gadgets specifically designed for no more cuts while opening cans. Most of them are less than a few hundred dollars, so there is literally nothing at all stopping you from having one of the best times anyone can possibly have, while consuming a can of raw dog food riddled with random horse parts.

Now, I know what you're thinking:

'I personally don't mind eating raw dog food riddled with random horse parts, but what about those readers of yours who are vegetarians or vegans?'

Dear beautiful readers, you amaze me. How selfless and generous of you to think about those people who choose to live different lifestyles to your own. I am not sure if you were always so heartfelt and caring, or if you have just learned those skills while reading this book, but I applaud you, and I am sure it will not surprise you at all when I tell you that of course I am not going to leave out vegetarians and vegans. I totally support their lifestyle decisions. And although this next game can be played by all, and is also very cheap, and very easy to enjoy, it was actually designed to be right smack up the vegetarian and vegan alley. This game is called:

Do you take coupons here?

Step One: Gather several people near the meat section in your local supermarket.

Step Two: See who can be the quickest to re-build a cow.

Step Three: No eating any cow while playing or you're disqualified (you're welcome my vegetarian and vegan players!)

Enjoy the future my Hell Yeah, awesomnessous friends! I love you all.

(Ps: Hint for game two – they hide the eyeballs in the dog food).

THE END

(That means there is literally nothing after this, right?)

Glossary of key terms

The End – A big fat lie, especially when trying to extradite yourself from a bad relationship.

Book - what you're reading, good for you for sticking with tradition.

Kindle - unless you're reading on one of these, good for you, embracing new technology.

Open-minded ness - seeking to understand and see the good on both sides of an argument, with no judgment. Something I possess in spades.

Kindle - I buy books on kindle too, but screw new technology, buy a book please, I'm begging you. New technology users are the disgrace of the modern world, please stick to the old methods, they were popular for a reason.

iPhone - what I wrote this glossary on.

Hope - something optimists use to make pessimists feel bad about themselves.

Chocolate Croissant – A delicious food option, seriously delicious.

Alphabetical order - a myth on what's correct popularized by ancient goat worshipping pagans.

Laziness - something easy to overcome with made up facts.

Salad dressing - a product that just came to my mind for some unknown reason.

City – A place you need good credentials to live in.

David Tieck - just some dude.

Dude - another word for 'amazing awesome super genius'.

Humbleness - something made up by God fearing nudists.

Cinderella - a story about gold diggers.

Gold diggers - hard working miners who battled horrible conditions, disease and endless physically draining work in the mere hope of striking precious metal aka - people who despise alternative meanings of terms, and who also hate women who will only sleep with you for money- except prostitutes, their only source of companionship, unless they strike gold where then for some reason they get all the women they want - we can all hope.

Hope - something optimists use to make pessimists feel bad about themselves.

Repetition - something that's awesome to fill up space.

It's all happening – a term used by people who don't know the definition of 'all'.

Anger - an emotion I never want to feel again, so don't fucking start anything alright?

Insomnia - a condition so bad sufferers should have carte blanch to murder anyone they want.

Happy couples - people who shouldn't be allowed out in public.

Ghost kitty who used to visit me - proof of an afterlife.

Kids - things people who have the time to read this probably don't have.

Shelf life - a game cockroaches who choose to live in hammer stores often regret playing.

Over bite - the correct way to have 'just one bite' of someone else's cake, you said I could have a bite, so why are you complaining you selfish prick.

Tennis - a sport invented by a particularly hairy blonde haired Swedish man who looked at his scrotum and thought 'I wouldn't mind hitting that with a racket'.

Love - something made up by happy people to torture those less fortunate.

Cynic - the best type of person imaginable.

Timing – Something that can only improve your life, depending on whether you do it good style or bad style, like say writing your glossary of key terms right after a bad break up is what's called 'good timing', where as having your first meal after surgery at the same time someone is playing 'Photo Finish' is what's called 'bad-timing'.

Farcicality weirdo pukes – The scientific study of ants.

BU:BBLES - Bubbles Union: Bubbles Believe Life Escalates Spectacularly. A real life, dead set true organisation that really does exist, I swear, Google it if you don't believe me.

Bang – An awesome type of sex act.

I know what you are thinking – demonstrations of my flawless psychic abilities.

Truth – Ok Brad Pitt didn't really write that letter from the future, but I am sure he'll be fine with the words and opinions I put in his mouth, right?

Abortion – A medical procedure that is desperately funny, well mostly to immature boys, well that is until they accidently knock someone up. Can anyone recommend a good vasectomist?

Acknowledgments Section - Something no book reader has ever read.

THE END
(For real this time)

Acknowledgments

Thanks to Goshie, for always inspiring me to 'go right on with it', while simultaneously somehow making my guest bathroom floor wet at all times. Thank you to Charlie Gelbart, for your love and support, and for inspiring me by being the funniest person I have ever met. Thank you to Cosmo for being the cutest, craziest most awesomenessous kitty ever. Thanks to Nathan 'the Vibe' Andrews, for your awesome music, and for inspiring me to follow my every whim, no matter how damaging they are to my body and soul. Thanks to all my other friends for putting up with a freak like me, one day I'll fulfill my promise and tell you a story or joke so gross it'll make one of you puke. To the rest of my mates I love you all so much that I am referring to you all collectively and anonymously in the section that no one reads, so you all owe me one, and I *will* be collecting, you can count on it. Thanks to my pet camel Carpet Mustard, the best friend a guy could have.

And a big special thanks to Nick 'Slinky' Day who somehow turns weird sketches of mine into book covers. I forgot to mention him as cover designer in the last book and man he whines about it, it's just whine whine whine, nothing but freaking whining – he's all like:

'Its ok Dave, I'm just honored you chose my design.'

And I'm like 'oh my God Nick, stop whining, besides if you're going to highjack this books foreword as friends of imaginary ex wives of imaginary kids of imaginary dictators I made up just to make people imaginary question your imaginary integrity then maybe I should be distancing myself from you anyway, you freaking whiner - your identical twin brother Andy is pretty cool though'.

And he's like 'You are truly an awesome human DT.'

And I'm like 'I get it, it's up to me to make *your* life awesome, it's up to me to make everyone's life awesome, God damn it, maybe if you stop putting pressure on me and stop whining all the time, I can get back to doing something about it – meanwhile go mop up the guest bathroom, for some reason there is *always* bloody water on the floor in there.'

THE END
(Thanks everyone)

Glossary of key terms continued...

Spelling and grammar and rules and the like – Things totally not worth the effort of getting perfect.

Effort – something best used for something good, like dragging on some awesomnessous joke about a book being over when there is still some book to go, not that I think anyone will read this far, wait maybe I should put in some sort of test to see if people actually do read this far?

Test – If you read this far, and find me online, you know at all the normal places, and message me with the following special code sentence, I will give you a thousand dollars – ok here it is, the special code message you should send me is:

> 'I am fully aware and completely understand that when David Tieck offered to send me a thousand dollars he was not being serious, and by sending this message to him I am making my position very clear that in no way do I ever expect David Tieck to send me money, nor do I even want him to, even if he did I would refuse to take it, and even if he insisted I would still refuse to take it, and if I ever try to take him to court to get money off him, I would like this message read out loud in the court, and for everyone to laugh at me for being so stupid as to think that David Tieck was actually, literally offering me a thousand dollars, PS I

wear underpants made for six year old boys because it makes me feel less stupid when I make doodoo in my pants'.

I will be awaiting your messages – wow, a thousand bucks up for grab, what are you going to buy first?

The Finale of Endingnessous: Hell Yeah!!!

Praise for David

"Original, acid, and wild...wacky writing par excellence"
The Los Angeles Times on David Sedaris

"The funniest damn writer in the whole country"
The Miami Herald on Dave Barry

"Achieved cineaste godhood and popular acclaim as a mastermind of mind-bending masterpieces"
Spin Magazine on David Lynch

"One of the most brilliant living comics"
Time Magazine on Dave Chappelle

"One of the most handsome men on the face of the planet"
Marie Claire on David Beckham

"Has Comic Power"
The Guardian on Dave Gorman

"Changed comedy forever"
Rolling Stone Magazine on Larry David

"The Best Late Night Talk Show Guy We've Ever Had"
Regis Philban on David Letterman

"Hilarious as expected. He's a master"

Artie Lange on David Spade

"Without David, popular music as we know it pretty much wouldn't exist"

Moby on David Bowie

"He is the minister of God to thee for good"

The Bible on King David of Jerusalem

"Can do more with one note than most other guitar players can do with the whole fret board"

David Mustaine on David Gilmour

"One of the best things I have ever read"

Tony Parsons on David Baddiel

"Is a fat fucking faggot"

School Bully on David Tieck

About the Author

David Tieck is an artist, actor and comedian from Sydney Australia. He is the author of *Losing My Virginity 52 Times*, and *The Embarrassing Memory Murderer*. Since discovering an eatery where you could build your own Sundaes, David went mad with power, and now spends his time hiding under his bed contemplating life and existence, while muttering to himself 'hot fudge or hot caramel, hot fudge or hot caramel' over and over.